Jainism for a New World C

Siddheshwar Rameshwar Bhatt

Jainism for a New World Order

Springer

Siddheshwar Rameshwar Bhatt
New Delhi, India

ISBN 978-981-33-4043-5 ISBN 978-981-33-4041-1 (eBook)
https://doi.org/10.1007/978-981-33-4041-1

This Springer imprint is published by the registered company Springer Nature Singapore Pte Ltd.
The registered company address is: 152 Beach Road, #21-01/04 Gateway East, Singapore 189721, Singapore

Dedicated to His Holiness Pujyashri Karshni Swami

(Dr.) Gurusharananandji Maharaj

Who is an embodiment of wisdom, affection and love

Foreword

Human race is going through unprecedented manyfold and multidimensional crises on almost every front of life. During last few centuries, scientific investigations and technological innovations have remained the dominant driving force behind every human endeavour. These two, together with purely economic model of development, seemed to make human life more comfortable, smoother, prosperous, healthier and happier. Man tried to emerge as the 'Master' of 'Nature', and the whole universe became sheer instrument for satisfying his boundless unending desires.

Gradually, the deeper implications and after effects of this model of growth started manifesting themselves in every sphere of human life. Environmental imbalance caused by unmindful excessive exploitation of natural resources resulted in dreadful natural calamities threatening the very survival of life on earth. Egocentric individualism, non-teleological gross materialism and consumption-oriented world view have led to collapse of major value structures in moral realm. Social institutions are disintegrating, and most of the political and economic organizations have lost their significance or have become defunct. In attempting to satiate unlimited desires from limited natural resources, each individual, community and nation have become competitor and enemy of every other and there is complete erosion of universal values of love, care, share, help compassion, mutual community binding, support, fellowship and harmony. Mad race for accumulating the weapons of mass destruction has brought human race at the verge of extinction. Physical and mental stress has engulfed the very spirit of humanity, weakening its enormous inner strength.

The question is what is the way out of this alarming situation? How do we deal with this scary scenario? Mere science and technology cannot resolve the problems largely caused by their own exclusive and excessive misuse. Perhaps, we need to go back to our ancient time-tested wisdom which always maintained beautiful balance between material and spiritual, physical and mental, individual and community, particular and universal, part and whole, relative and absolute, and empirical and transcendental. Our contemporary problems, conflicts and strives may find their solution in the profound thoughts of our ancient sages, seers and seekers of truth. We need to dive a little deeper in the vast ocean of Indian philosophical and cultural tradition so that we may come up with practical and concrete solutions to the major issues bothering human civilizations at this juncture.

This is precisely what Prof. S. R. Bhatt has done in the present book *Jainism and New World Order*. He has addressed the most crucial contemporary issues from the perspective of Jain philosophical tradition and has tried to show how its holistic vision and an innovative understanding of its foundational principles can provide effective, efficacious and pragmatic solutions to our present-day ailments. He has creatively re-examined the basic tenets of Jainism and with his in-depth analysis has demonstrated how an honest genuine adherence to these can create a happy symbiosis of material prosperity and spiritual enhancement.

Professor S. R. Bhatt is one of the most learned distinguished scholars of Indian philosophical, cultural and religious tradition. His vast knowledge and deep understanding of all the philosophical systems of India is reflected in the large number of books and research papers authorized by him. His comprehensive vision and holistic approach for resolving problematic issues is exhibited in this book also, where along with presenting Jain perspective, he has enriched the analysis by providing Vedic–Upanishadic, Buddhistic, Advaita Vedantic and Gandhian perspectives.

Chapter 1 of the book presents an insightful exposition of the key concepts of Jain metaphysics, epistemology and ethics. A brief but precise account of Jain theory of Reality (*utpāda vyāya dhrovya yuktam sat—guṇa paryāya vad dravyam*), *Anekāntvāda* (*anant dharmātkam vastu*), *Śyādvāda* (the theory of relativity of human perception and expression) and five cardinal virtues—*ahiṃsā, satya, asteya, aparigraha and brahmacarya*—prepares a perfect background for analysing multidimensional contemporary problems. Here, the author rightly emphasizes the practical orientation of Jain philosophy by referring to the first sutra of Tattvārtha-Sūtra (the most accepted foundational Jain text) S*amyagdarśanjñānacāritranimokṣamargah*, according to which liberation from all sufferings is possible only when right belief and right knowledge are translated into right conduct.

Chapter 2 deals with the most glaring problem of our times—environmental imbalance. The author believes that the root cause of all environmental pollution is human misuse of freedom and lack of the sense of responsibility. This pollution is primarily caused by the mental and intellectual human perversions, which get reflected on the external physical level.

The anthropocentric world view that man is the centre of the cosmos and hence is the master of everything (animate or inanimate) has made us painfully self-centred, insensitive and devoid of any feeling of responsibility, fellowship, concern, love, care and compassion. Undoubtedly, human being is the highest emergent in the cosmic process so far and as rational agent is capable of controlling and making changes in the external environment with the help of science and technology. But the human identity, the author says, cannot be defined in isolation of other beings and elements of the cosmos. The famous Jain dictum *paraspaograham jivanam* highlights this organismic, interdependent, interconnected, multilayered nature of human existence.

Unlike utilitarian, materialist and mechanical ecology propagated by West, Jainism advocates 'deep ecology', which is essentially spiritual, teleological, holistic and integral in character. Since environmental degradation even at physical level is caused by deluded egocentric individualistic mindset, to cure this ill the remedial measures must also be sought in the transformation of this mindset. To accomplish this, the author suggests some important steps from Jain perspective. Nature must be approached with a sense of respect and gratitude, and besides its instrumental worth, its intrinsic value must be realized. *Ahiṃsā*, the highest cardinal virtue of Jain ethics, is based on its metaphysical principle of equality of all living beings. According to Jain texts, not only humans but all animals (non-human creatures), plants and even earth, water, fire and air are also living beings and have soul. Every soul is potentially capable of attaining the highest knowledge (*kevala jñāna*) and ultimate liberation (*mokṣa*) by gradual removal of ignorance (*avidyā*). Due to strong belief in the universal equality of all living beings, Jain ethics not only defines *ahiṃsā* as non-killing or non-harming other living beings but also prescribes for giving due opportunities to them for self-preservation and self-development. Love, compassion, kindness, the feeling of fellowship and friendliness naturally become primary virtues in such a value framework. *aparigraha*—minimizing of possessions, desires, wants and consumptions—is another important Jain doctrine which can immensely help in improving external as well as internal mental environment.

The principles of *ahiṃsā* and *aparigraha* joined with the doctrines of (*asteya*) non-stealing and *anekanta* can bring a radical paradigm shift in our economic planning and execution, and the author believes it will lead us to the era of relative, regenerative and compassionate economics. According to him, there is an urgent need to transform our existing value structure and Jain principles can play pivotal role in this restructuring. Education systems based on Jain values and code of conduct can create a genuine environmental consciousness and help in regaining environmental balance.

Ahiṃsā is considered to be the supreme virtue in Indian cultural and religious ethos. Jainism believes it to be the foundation of all other virtues and the highest duty of human beings (*Ahiṃsāparmodharmaḥ*). The importance of *ahiṃsā* in building a new world order cannot be overemphasized. Therefore, the learned author has devoted Chap. 3 of the book exclusively for the analysis of its various aspects and practical implications of its application.

In its grammatical formulation, *ahiṃsā* appears to be a negative term, but it has deep positive connotation and the author has rightly highlighted it in the context of Jain code of conduct (*ācāra śāstra*). Refraining from killing, harming, torturing, enslaving, exploiting, oppressing, insulting or abusing any living being is only one aspect of *ahiṃsā*. Love, compassion, care, cooperation, coexistence, peace, friendship and harmony are also integral part of its constitution. And therefore, practice of *ahiṃsā* is not limited to certain don'ts (*niṣedha*). It also involves active engagement in certain positive actions. Not killing or not harming any existent is necessary but not sufficient condition for being *ahiṃsaka*. For that, one has to engage in selfless service to others and make efforts to improve living conditions and quality of life of every creature on earth. To this comprehensive conception of *ahiṃsā*, Jainism adds another important dimension. It maintains that *hiṃsā* in any form, even from mind, body or speech, is not acceptable. Thus, not only physical, but also mental and verbal *hiṃsā* is prohibited. Strict adherence to these rules makes Jainism the most rigorous advocate of non-violence.

But this conception of non-violence supports neither withdrawal from positive action nor any kind of cowardice. In consistency with its practical approach, Jain scriptures mention four types of *hiṃsā*: (1) *ārambhi*—the minimum unavoidable *hiṃsā* involved in performing daily routine works; (2) *udyogi*—*hiṃsā* necessary for certain occupations and professions such as agriculture and mining; (3) *virodhajā*—*hiṃsā* used in self-defence against violent attacks by enemies or cruel creatures; and (4) *sankalpika*—intentional and deliberate *hiṃsā* which is unnecessary and is avoidable. The first three kinds of *hiṃsā* are permitted with the condition that it must be minimum, unavoidable and justified. But the fourth kind of *hiṃsā* is completely prohibited.

Ahiṃsā as an intrinsic value, and a sublime ideal is integrally related to all other fundamental principles of Jainism. The author explains its intimate relationship with *anekāntavāda*, the law of karma, truth, *aparigraha*, equality, happiness, peace, friendship, forgiveness, vegetarianism, physical and mental health and ecology. As a guiding principle of economy, it ensures non-violent, non-exploitative process of production, distribution and consumption and thus paves way for sustainable development.

Like *ahiṃsā*, *aparigraha* (the principle of non-possessiveness) is another fundamental dictum of Jainism. It is one of the five mandatory vows (*pañca mahāvrata*). Jain saints like Acharya Mahapragya place it even higher than *ahiṃsā* because possessiveness invariably causes violence. In his view, the ideal of a non-violent society can be actualized only by strictly following the principle of non-possessiveness.

Umaswati in Tattvārtha-sūtra (7.12) defines *parigraha* as *murcchā*, the tendency to cling to objects (animate or inanimate) in order to satisfy unlimited, insatiable desires. *Aparigraha* is practice of abstaining from all kinds of possessions, both internal and external. It implies minimizing of desires, wants, needs, accumulation of goods and put control on greed and attachment. According to Jain thinkers, unrestrained possessiveness necessarily leads to economic disparity, deprivation, exploitation, consumerism, wasteful expenditure, violence, hatred, jealousy and different kinds of heinous crimes. In Chap. 4 of the book, various benefits of *aparigraha* are explained. And it is argued that adherence to the principle of non-possession ensures ecological equilibrium, sustainable development, absence of class conflict, global peace and prosperity and, above all, intragenerational and intergenerational justice.

An important implication of principle of *ahiṃsā* (live and let live) is manifested in the form of strong advocacy for strict vegetarianism in Jain (*ācāra-śāstra*) code of conduct. Purity of food is highly emphasized in Jainism, and it is believed that any food produced/obtained by killing or harming any living being not only affects health of human body and mind adversely but is also non-conducive for spiritual progress. Jains are expected to follow strict dietary restrictions, have to avoid even vegetarian food, which is *tāmasic* in character, and are not supposed to consume alcohol and even honey. For health reasons and in order to avoid killing of insects and microorganisms, they have to abstain from eating after sunset and are encouraged to keep fasting at regular intervals. The learned author in Chap. 5 of the book has given an interesting account of enormous benefits of vegetarianism and has very convincingly shown how it can be used to deal with modern-day problems related to physical, mental and spiritual health.

As stated earlier, value erosion and loss of faith in moral and spiritual order is one of the most troublesome problems of our times. Prevalence of violence, indiscipline, selfishness and crimes are all its resultants. In Chap. 6, the author suggests that the pathway to deal with the situation of value entropy is self-purification and spiritual realization, which can be accomplished only through character-oriented right kind of education. In his view, Jain concept of *samvara* (stoppage of karmic inflow which causes bondage) and *nirjarā* (destruction of accumulated karma) helps in eradication of vices and promoting a virtuous life. This chapter also discusses problem of religious fundamentalism and terrorism, and the author maintains that the Jain concept of *anekānta* (the theory of multiplicity of perspectives and relative truth) can play a significant role in building mutual respect and understanding among followers of different religions. Study of comparative religions must be encouraged, and instead of religious education, education about religions must be promoted.

Relationship between science, religion and spirituality is another intriguing issue of contemporary times. Dealing with it in Chap. 7, the author maintains that these three have distinct areas of operation and there is no antagonism among them. Science deals with empirical, physical/material reality, while religion and spirituality are concerned with higher dimensions of our consciousness. Science and the technology based on it have phenomenally improved the quality of life on earth. But its self-acclaimed value neutrality has also caused tremendous catastrophes endangering the very existence of life on earth. Science advancing under spiritualistic guidance can serve the purpose of both material prosperity (*abhyudaya*) and spiritual enhancement (*niḥśreyasa*). But for that, religion also has to free itself from sectarianism, fundamentalism, dogmatism and fanaticism. It has to open itself for fresh new ideas and harmonious outlook. There is no unbridgeable cleavage between the two. To take the benefit of both, all we need to do is to spiritualize science and make religion and spirituality scientific. For achieving this goal, the author believes the Jain technique of *prekṣā dhyāna* (developed by Acharya Tulsi and Acharya Mahapragya) can be highly useful because according to them, it is based on synthesis of science and spirituality.

In continuity of the earlier discussion, Chap. 8 addresses the issue of religious harmony and tolerance at greater length. Plurality of religions is an undeniable reality. Possibility of one single universal religion is in fact a far-fetched idea. We have to learn to coexist with multiplicity of religions. Here again, Jain theory of *anekānta* and *syādvāda* can be immensely helpful in cultivating a mindset, which accepts equality of all religions perceiving every religion as one *naya*—an alternative approach to the truth. This results in mutual respect and appreciation and creates environment of harmony, love, peace and tolerance among followers of different religions. This precisely is the essence of Indian secularism.

We are living in an era marked with fiery debates on clash of civilizations and conflicts of cultures. Cultures are carriers of comprehensive world view embodying a specific value structure, which manifests itself in the form of tradition. These days, establishing cultural dominance and destroying or demeaning other cultures is becoming alarmingly prevalent. In its known history of 5000 years, India has successfully preserved cultural pluralism and has encouraged coexistence of different cultures. As in the case of multiplicity of religions, the Jain theory of *anekāntavāda* provides guidelines to deal with this situation also. The idea of coexistence of multiple, sometimes even contrary viewpoints (*naya*) definitely encourages acceptance and respect for plurality of cultures. Chapter 9 of the book presents an elaborate discussion on this phenomenon.

Economy constitutes one of the basic pillars, which shape and deeply influence human life on earth. In the present age of globalization, economic structures are becoming more and more individualistic, materialistic, competitive, consumerist and simply profit seeking. In Chap. 10, the author points to the need of a paradigm shift and presents the idea of spiritual globalization based on Jain principles of *ahiṃsā*, *asteya*, *aparigraha*, *śubha*, *lābha* and *icchā-parimāṇa* (limiting desires). This can pave the way for cooperative, compassionate, non-consumerist, sustainable model of economy which will be able to cure many ills of our present-day financial systems.

Political structure of any society to a large extent determines its sociocultural and economic structure. History has witnessed several forms of political organizations such as monarchy, oligarchy, aristocracy, autocracy, democracy, dictatorship, totalitarianism, socialism, communism and many more. Among all the above, democracy, almost unanimously, is considered to be the best form of governance. With its foundational principle—'Government of the people, by the people and for the people', it is supposed to promote people's participation, rule of law, human dignity and spirit of fellowship. But in its actual functioning, the author believes presently it is suffering with incurable drawbacks, deficiencies and deformities. Hence, there is an urgent need to re-examine its postulates and propose an alternative model of governance, which retains merits of democracy but is free from its weakness. In Chap. 11, the author suggests that this new model can be developed in the light of foundational principles of Indian tradition in general and Jain ethics in particular. Based on the notion of organic harmony, this new form of political organization can be termed as 'Dharmocracy' or 'Dharmatantra' in which the rule of 'Dharma' is given the supreme status.

Chapter 12 is devoted to the analysis of Jain theory of *puruṣārtha*. There is a general acceptance of the scheme of fourfold *puruṣārtha* (the goals of all human endeavours) in Indian culture. These are *dharma, artha, kāma* and *mokṣa*. Remaining well within this scheme, Jainism adds a significant dimension to the notion of *puruṣārtha* by taking the theory of karma to its logical conclusion. It does not believe in the idea of a creator, sustainer, personal God. The universe according to its metaphysics is strictly governed by the law of karma. Man is his own making.

His past, present and future are completely determined by fruits of his own actions. In the absence of possibility of any kind of divine intervention, self-effort is the only way for redemption from sufferings and attaining desirable goals at individual or societal level. This strict adherence to the law of karma makes Jainism truly a religion of self-help, *puruṣārtha.* The author has presented an interesting exposition of its various aspects in this chapter.

Human existence on this earth appears to be beset with ignorance (*mithyātva*) and consequent bondage, miseries, delusions and imperfections. Man seems to suffer from innumerable limitations and finitude. But this Jainism believes is not his true nature. Human soul is abode of infinite knowledge, infinite bliss and infinite power. It has potential to transcend all kinds of limitations—physical, mental, emotional or intellectual. It is even beyond the boundaries of space and time. It is intrinsically pure and perfect. The ultimate goal of human life is to realize this true nature of self.

According to Jainism, souls have three states of existence: (1) conditional and embodied soul called *bahirātmā* or the physical self which identifies itself with physical body and material objects; (2) awakened and indwelling soul called *antarātmā* or the interior self which discriminates itself from the body and sense organs and renouncers all identification with animate or inanimate objects; and (3) pure and supreme soul called *paramātmā*—the transcendental self which is perfect, omniscient, omnipotent and free from all karmic bondages. The summum bonum of human life is attainment of the state of *paramātmā*. It is a journey from the state of exterior self to the state of transcendental self, through the intermediary stage of interior self.

Jain theory of *guṇasthāna* lays down the details of the fourteen stages through which human soul can gradually move upward—from imperfection to perfection, from bondage to freedom, from suffering to infinite bliss. In the final chapter of the book, the author has presented a lucid account of this process and has explained how through reflective awareness, self-consciousness, yoga and meditation, the empirical self can get transformed into transcendental self—the terminus of all human endeavours.

I feel privileged and honoured in writing the foreword of the book authored by a visionary scholar like Prof. S. R. Bhatt. Reading this book was a joyful journey. With his holistic approach, the author has analysed various dimensions of human life—personal, social, political, economical, environmental, religious, moral and spiritual as well. Though the main focus of the book is to present the Jain perspective, in-depth knowledge and understanding of the learned author of other systems of Indian philosophical tradition has enormously enriched the discussion. He has addressed the major problems of our contemporary times and has tried to respond by rational and creative reinterpretation of basic foundational principles of Jainism. With his remarkable conceptual clarity and refreshing new insights, this book will contribute significantly in improving knowledge and understanding of traditional wisdom and will inspire further research in this direction. Besides being useful for serious scholars, this book, I believe, will arouse interest of common readers also towards exploring the deeper dimensions of human existence and will help in creating a new world order free from major ills of our present-day scenario.

Prof. Kusum Jain
Director, Prakrit Bharati Academy
Jaipur, India

Head, Department of Philosophy

Former Dean, Faculty of Arts

Director, P. G. School of Humanities

Director, U. G. C. Centre of Advanced
Studies in Philosophy

Principal, University Maharani College
Jaipur, India

Preface

The objective of this book is both academic and practical. It analyses some glaring global issues with a holistic vision and pragmatic solution from Jain perspective. The maxim 'Think globally and act locally' is the guiding principle. So, there has to be two-pronged attempt—theoretical exposition and collaborative practical venture. This work is a blueprint for individual development, social transformation and cosmic well-being on the basis of basic tenets and practices of Jainism. I have presented an innovative understanding of the basic premises, doctrines and tenets of Jainism as per the present-day needs and aspirations. That is why I have given contemporary thinking by way of background. For this purpose, I have also drawn out necessary implications from the Jain literature. It is my belief that Jainism is as relevant today as it was in the past. Its salient message and needful practices have global significance, provided they are properly understood and genuinely practised for cosmic wellness. Dissemination of awareness about them and social services as their practical counterparts are the modalities to be adopted. It is no doubt a herculean task as the arena is very vast and not easily manageable, but the task is needed and important. The aim is to motivate people and to guide them for such activities as they are conducive to universal peace and amity, global prosperity and harmony. Though this is lofty ideal, it can be achieved gradually and persistently in a programmatic action. In all human enterprises, there has to be a happy symbiosis of material prosperity and spiritual enhancement. Then only, there can be universal peace and harmony.

There can be many alternative ways to realize this goal. All may be effective and efficacious, but the Jain approach is more suitable to the contemporary needs and aspirations. The Jain theories of *Anekānta*, and *syādvāda*, clear demarcation between niścaya (trans-worldly) and *vyavahāra* (worldly) and principles of *Mahāvrata* and *Aṇuvrata* need to be propagated and practised at the global level in a systematic and methodical way. The exposal of some glaring issues outlined in this work provides the justification and need for undertaking such activities to go to the root causes rather than attending to outer symptoms. The Jain community has the required wherewithal, will and zeal, and therefore such an enterprise can be undertaken unifiedly without sectarian considerations under its mentorship. This has been the message of Revered Tīrthankaras, and undertaking this task is real worship, adoration and tribute to them.

There are myriads of problems in the world which demand immediate solutions. There is a spread of violence all around giving rise to conflict situations—individual, familial, communal, international, etc., there is environmental degradation resulting in many types of illness, there are psychosomatic diseases, socio-economic inequalities and misuse of scientific and technological capabilities, and the list is unending. One of the major causes for this is lack of moral and spiritual development because of the absence of proper education. This also requires transvaluation of our value perception. For all these, Jain perspectives on different issues may be helpful.

In order to approach and solve global issues, there is a need of paradigm shift in our value perception and for this purpose the Jain view is highly relevant and efficacious. The objective of this book is to state the Jain view towards right modes of thinking *(samyak jñāna)* and harmonious ways of living *(samyak cāritra)* as efficacious means to solve problems humankind is facing today.

This book is an outcome of my studies in Jainism. In this book, some ideas and statements are repeated for the sake of connectivity and emphasis but this seems to be necessary. For the sake of smooth and non-bothersome reading, I have used textual references to the minimum but have given a list of suggested readings and bibliography.

New Delhi, India

Siddheshwar Rameshwar Bhatt

Acknowledgements

In writing this book, I have been inspired by His Holiness Late Acharya Shri Mahapragyaji. Following his Guru Acharya Shri Tulsiji, he pondered over most of the contemporary problems and suggested genuine solutions. I remember him with reverence and gratitude for encouraging me to study Jainism. I am only expanding his ideas. I am thankful to Jain Vishva Bharati Institute for providing me grant on the project 'Engaging Jainism with Modern Issues'. In preparing this book, I have been benefitted from the same. For this, I am grateful to the Vice Chancellor of the university and to Prof. (Dr.) Samani Chaitanya Pragya who gave valuable suggestions and guided me. I express my gratitude to Prof. Kusum Jain, an erudite Jain scholar, Director of Prakrit Academy, Jaipur, for writing Foreword to this book. I am indebted to all the scholars from whose books I have learnt quite a lot. I thank Ms. Vandana Sharma for helping me in going through the manuscript and putting diacritical marks on Sanskrit expressions. I also express my gratitude to Ms. Satvinder Kaur for encouraging me to write and undertaking this publication on behalf of Springer Nature. I dedicate this book to His Holiness Pujyashri Swami Gurusharananadaji Maharaj, who like Ācārya Haribhadra cherishes equal respect for all religions. He is an embodiment of wisdom and prudence, love and compassion, fellowship and benevolence.

Siddheshwar Rameshwar Bhatt

Table of Diacritical Marks

Key to Transliteration (Using Diacritical Marks)

अ	इ	उ	ऋ
a	i	u	ṛ

आ	ई	ऊ	ए	ऐ	ओ	औ	अं	अःa
ā	ī	ū	e	ai	o	au	aṃ	aḥ

Classified Consonants

क	ख	ग	घ	ङ
k	kh	g	gh	ṅ

च	छ	ज	झ	ञ
c	ch	j	jh	ñ

ट	ठ	ड़	ढ	ण
ṭ	ṭh	ḍ	ḍh	ṇ

त	थ	द	ध	न
t	th	d	dh	n

प	फ	ब	भ	म	म् (apropriate)
p	ph	b	bh	m	ṃ

Unclassified Consonants

य	र	ल	व	श	ष	स	ह	क्ष	त्र	ज्ञ
Y	r	l	v	Ś	ṣ	s	h	kṣa	tra	jña

Anusvaraḥ-(·) ⇨	ṁ
Visargaḥ-(:) ⇨	ḥ

Opinions on the Book

Opinion 1

The book "*Jainism for New World Order*" is timely and a very valuable addition to the knowledge about Jain Dharma; one of the oldest religions of the world.

I admire the depth and clarity in this book by a highly respected and acclaimed Jain scholar who in spite of the fact that he was not born in the Jain tradition and still produced such a beautiful and unbiased piece of literary work.

Over the years, I have noticed that most of the Indian authors will quote, give references and bibliography generally of Indian authors only and similarly the Western authors will give Western references only but not in this book. This book is well balanced with Indian and Western references and contains a very vast bibliography. This is very helpful for future study and research in Jainism by scholars.

One remarkable feature of this book is that it is not just for theoreticians, philosophers and academician only. It is for all those who are eager to know about Jain Dharma. Each topic and subject in this book has been discussed from multifaceted and multidimensional angles and viewpoints such as social relevance, inevitability, impact (desirable and not desirable), scientific and technical aspects and relevance, pluralism, secularism, globalization and its impact, coexistence, tradition (*parampara*) *anekanta* perspective, cultural pluralism, comparison with other philosophies , beliefs, social, political, human health, economics, ecology, environment, conflict resolution, modern society, political and many more. This alone makes this book very valuable and a great source of knowledge.

(Right now, the whole world is gripped with the outbreak of Coronavirus which continues to sow tragedy on countless scale. Many lives have been lost, the economies world over have been turned upside down and life as we have known has been dramatically altered. In this context, several thousand years ago, Jainism preached the concept of *Parasparopagrahajivānām*. What it means is that none of us can live the journey of life alone. For the first time, due to the threat from this common enemy, there is a realization that we all are inter-dependent, interconnected, in fact entangled with each and have co-existence with each other. Truly, we are inseparable and that we support each other. Our very survival is dependent on each other and on the rest of the world.) The author in this book very clearly and lucidly explains the relevance of Jain Dharma in this time of great epidemic and that Jain Dharma is not merely a view of the world but a way of life based on it. This is a MUST to read book.

Sulekh C. Jain Ph.D
Past President Federation of Jain Associations
in North America (JAINA) and Chairman
JAINA Academic Liaison Committee,
Las Vegas, Nevada, USA

Opinion 2

Enhanced scientific and technological research is having serious effects on Human beings in their search for ultimate truth and happiness at both personal and global levels as it is resulting in our material well-being with simultaneous adverse effects on our value schema in the form of inequality, intolerance, aggression, greater stress, life style problems for individuals accompanied with dreadful terrorism, excessive consumption, fast depletion of natural resources and global warming.

This book by Prof.Bhatt is a welcome gift to all who intend to address these developments as it provides a well-reasoned and systematic blue print for individual development, social transformation, cosmic well-being and ultimate perfection based on time tested tenets and practices of Jainism starting with definition of reality, self and non-self, leading to lifestyle practices based on of *Ahimsā, Aparigraha, Anekāanta* and Self -effort and conflict resolution.

I congratulate Prof.Bhatt for this great work.

Dr. Shugan C. Jain
Chairman
International School for Jain Studies

Contents

1 **Jain View Towards Right Modes of Thinking and Harmonious Ways of Living** 1
Introduction 1
Relevance of Jain Philosophy 2
Jain View of Cosmic Process 2
Uniqueness of Jain Philosophy 3
Symbiosis of Local and Global Thaught 4
Multiple Approaches to Reality 4
Practical Orientation of Jain Philosophy (*Darśana*) 5
Importance of Proper Knowledge (*Samyak Jñāna*) 6
Nature of Reality 8
Concepts of *Dravya, Guṇa* and *Paryāya* 8
Theories of *Naya* and *Saptabhaṅgīnaya* 9
Anekāntavāda and *Samatva* 11
Implications of *Anekāntavāda* 11
Importance of *Ahimsā* 12
Jain Theory of Management 12
Conclusion 13
References 15

2 **Jain Ethics, Environmental Crises and Remedial Measures** 17
Introduction 17
Human Being as Highest Emergent 18
Human Being as Rational, Free and Responsible Agent 18
Human Being Responsible for Environmental Pollution 19
Significance of Health and Hygiene 19
Genesis of All Problems 20
Need for Ethics and Morality 20
Cosmo-Centric Global Eco-Ethics 21
Panpsychism 22

Life of Collectivity . . . 22
Engaged Jainism . . . 23
Jain View of Surface Ecology and Deep Ecology . . . 23
Remedial Measures . . . 24
Conclusion . . . 28
References . . . 28

3 *Ahimsā* as Overriding Principle of Jain Ethos . . . 31
Introduction . . . 31
Need for *Ahimsā* . . . 32
Causes of Violence . . . 32
Ahimsā in Jainism . . . 33
Nature of *Ahimsā* . . . 33
Ahimsā Is Integral and Comprehensive . . . 34
Ahimsā Is Instinctive and Intrinsic . . . 34
Ahimsā Is Indivisible . . . 34
Ahimsā and Service (*Sevā*) to Others . . . 35
Ahimsā Is not Cowardice . . . 35
Himsā Is Sin . . . 35
Types of *Himsā* . . . 36
Ahimsā and Cognate or Allied Terms . . . 36
Ahimsā and *Anekānta* . . . 36
Ahimsā and Law of *Karma* . . . 37
Ahimsā and Truth . . . 37
Ahimsā and Equality . . . 37
Ahimsā and Happiness . . . 38
Ahimsā and Peace . . . 38
Peace and Sustainable Development . . . 38
Ahimsā and Friendship . . . 39
Ahimsā and Conflict Resolution . . . 40
Ahimsā and Harming Others . . . 40
Ahimsā and Forgiveness . . . 40
Ahimsā and Health Care . . . 41
Ahimsā and Vegetarianism . . . 42
Ahimsā and Ecology . . . 43
Ahimsā and *Aparigraha* . . . 43
Ahimsā and Economic Policy . . . 43
Three Guiding Principles of *Ahimsā* . . . 44
Remedial Measures . . . 44
References . . . 45

4 *Aparigraha*—As a Mode of Balanced Life 47
Introduction 47
Definition of *Aparigraha* 48
Causes of Possessiveness 48
Consequences of Possessiveness 49
Remedy 49
Need and Greed 49
Charity and Philonthrophy 50
Benefits of *aparigraha* 50
References 51

5 Vegetarianism: A Preferred Diet 53
Introduction 53
Importance of Human Body 54
Types of Body 54
Vital Energies and Diet 55
Necessity of Food 55
Healthy Diet 56
Fasting as Conducive to Health 56
Avoidance of Food Late in Night 57
Diseases due to Food 57
Science of Nutrition 58
Basic Elements of Food 58
Why Non-vegetarianism Should Be Rejected? 59
Vegetarianism as Disease Deterrent 59
Advantages of Vegetarian Food 60
Vegetarianism: Environment Protecting Food 61
Vegetarianism and Non-violence 61
Vegetarianism Cheaper from Economic Point of View 61
Health Is National Treasure 62
Why to Adopt Vegetarianism? 62
Training in Non-violence 63
Conclusion 63
Suggested Readings 64

6 Ethics of Knowledge, Value Entropy and Terrorism 65
Introduction 65
Value Entropy in Human Nature 66
Samyak Cāritra as Basis of Jain Ethics 66
Causes for Value Entropy 66
Role of Knowledge and Education 67
Menace of Terrorism 68
Jain Ethics as a Panacea for Religious Fundamentalism and Violence 69

Jain Ethics a Means to Self-realization . . . 69
Suggested Readings . . . 70

7 **Science, Religion and Spirituality** . . . 71
Introduction . . . 71
Science Explained . . . 72
Advantages of Science . . . 72
Limitations of Science . . . 73
Science and Technology not Value Neutral . . . 73
Role of Religion . . . 74
Misuse of Religion . . . 75
Science and Religion Have to Go Hand in Hand . . . 76
Spirituality Explained . . . 76
Science and Spirituality . . . 79
Spirituality and Science—Partners for Peace, Plenitude and Perfection . . . 80
References . . . 82

8 **Jain Perspective on Harmony of Religions and Religious Tolerance** . . . 85
Introduction . . . 85
Real Meaning of Religion . . . 86
Need for Religion . . . 86
Social Dimension of Religion . . . 87
Inevitability of Religion . . . 87
Desirable Impact of Religion . . . 87
Equability of All Religions . . . 88
Religion and Sect . . . 88
Religious Pluralism . . . 89
Religious Pluralism and Secularism in India . . . 90
Importance of Comparative Religious Studies . . . 91
References . . . 92

9 **Jain Model of Cultural Encounters, Confluences and Coexistence** . . . 93
Introduction . . . 93
Culture as All-Round Development . . . 93
Values and Culture . . . 94
Culture and Tradition . . . 94
Diversity of Human Existence and Culture . . . 95
Cultural Pluralism . . . 95
Indian Scene of Cultural Pluralism . . . 96

Conclusion 97
Suggested Readings 98

10 Role of Jainism in Evolving a New Paradigm of Global Economy 99
Introduction 99
Need for Paradigm Shift 100
Jain Model of Economy 101
Compassionate Economy 102
Regenerative Economics 102
Need for Cosmic Vision 103
Suggested Readings 103

11 Rethinking Democracy and a Plea for Dharmocracy 105
Introduction 106
Different Types of Democracy 106
Defects of Democracy 106
People's Participation 108
Rule of Majority 109
Rule of Law 109
Human Dignity 110
Fellowship 110
Democracy in Function 111
Jain Viewpoint 111
References 114

12 Jain Theory of *Puruṣārtha* 117
Introduction 117
Theory of *Pañcasamavāya* 118
Theory of *Karma* 119
Analysis of Concept of *Puruṣa* (Person) 120
Suggested Readings 122

13 Jain View of Perfection 123
Introduction 123
Organismic Approach to Reality 124
Nature of the Universe 125
Nature of Human Existence 125
Holistic Understanding 126
Progress as Evolution (:) Banking on Tradition and Rooted in Culture 127
Goal of Human Life and the Cosmic Process 128
Need of Global Human Endeavour 128
Quality of Life and Spiritual Globalization (Vasudhaiva Kuṭumbakam) 129

Mode of Achieving the Goal 130
Value Schema for Individual and Social Progress 130
Holistic and Integral Approach to Progress 131
Science, Technology and Social Progress 131
Appendix 132
Further Readings 134

Glossary 135

Bibliography 141

About the Author

Siddheshwar Rameshwar Bhatt (S. R. Bhatt) is an eminent philosopher and Sanskritist. Presently, he is a National Fellow of Indian Council of Social Science Research, Government of India. (He is presently the Chairman of Indian Philosophical Congress, Asian Philosophical Congress and Association of Indian Philosophers International. He is also the Former Chairman of the Indian Council of Philosophical Research, MHRD.). He retired as Professor and Head, Department of Philosophy, University of Delhi, Delhi. He is internationally known as an authority on ancient Indian culture, Buddhism, Jainism and Vedanta. His research areas include Indian philosophy, logic, epistemology, ethics, value theory, philosophy of education, philosophy of religion, comparative religion, social and political thought, etc. He has lectured in many universities and research institutes of the USA, Canada, Finland, Trinidad, North Korea, South Korea, Japan, China, Vietnam, Sri Lanka, Singapore and Thailand. He is a member of many national and international associations. He is a member of Board of Advisors of Council for Research in Values and Philosophy, Washington D.C., USA, which has brought out 300 volumes on world cultures and civilizations.

Chapter 1
Jain View Towards Right Modes of Thinking and Harmonious Ways of Living

Abstract The contemporary existential scenario, with all its ills and evils, demands serious attention to undertake its in-depth analysis and find remedial measures to rectify the prevailing melancholy situation. Here, Jainism can be of help to provide a blueprint for the elimination of present-day ailments. Jain thought with its holistic philosophy of interdependence, reciprocity, mutual care and share, universal love and compassion, fellowship and participation can offer an effective and more beneficial alternative to the present-day individualistic, materialistic, competitive and consumerist view of life and Reality. There are some seminal ideas, ideals and guiding principles contained here which may redeem humanity from its present plight.

Keywords *Anekāntavāda* · *Nayavāda* · *Saptabhaṇgī Naya* · *Ratnatraya* · *Paryāya* · *Ahimsā* · *Asteya* · *Aparigraha* · *Samvāda*

Introduction

As we acutely feel, all is not well with the contemporary existential scenario and this calls for a paradigm shift in our value perceptions, in our modes of thinking and ways of living. We are passing through a critical period struggling between the best possibilities and worst possibilities. At the present juncture, humankind is facing a crisis which is manifold and multidimensional. Human existence is stationed at a crossroad. It is a time when forces of unity and harmony should triumph, and marvels of science and technology can be used to ameliorate human suffering and ensure quality of life; precisely at this time, forces of terror and violence and impulses of lower human nature are advancing menacingly on a global scale. The ratiocinative human mind is aghast and confronted with a dilemma as to how to respond to the present scenario. Rationality in which humanity has placed great trust for realization of its ideals of true knowledge, virtuous conduct and authentic existence appears to have been overtaken by hurricane of unreason and blind faith and basal passions. It has therefore become imperative to explore deeper and higher dimensions of human resources by means of which we can successfully work for the victory of the ideals and values which have inspired onwards march of civilizations. Moving ahead in twenty-first century with rich, diverse and varied heritage, humankind is still searching for

S. R. Bhatt, *Jainism for a New World Order*,
https://doi.org/10.1007/978-981-33-4041-1_1

new paradigms, looking for new insights, novel intuitions and fresh approaches and therefore there is a need for serious 'rethinking' on the part of knowledgeable persons all over the world. There is a wide spread misapprehension about the nature and meaning of Reality and human existence, and consequently there is all-round global erosion of values, loss of dignity and authenticity in life, and predominance of disvalues masquerading as true values.

Relevance of Jain Philosophy

Jain philosophy being a systematic and critical reflection on our lived experiences, like all other systems of Indian philosophical thought, has the avowed task of providing a way out from this labyrinth with its liberating wisdom, and therefore it is the onus of responsibility on those who are exposed to Jain modes of thinking and ways of living to put forth fresh thinking and newer pathways by way of creative interpretations of Jain teachings and their faithful and sincere adherence, and come out with innovative paradigms to guide humanity. There is a need to address the imminent problems facing the humankind and provide genuine, effective and efficacious solutions failing which the rich and varied Jain culture will cease to be relevant to contemporary needs and aspirations and it may just remain an article of faith and one of the modes of worship.

Against this background, it is hoped that Jain thought, which is at once both ancient and contemporary, with its rationalistic philosophy of interdependence, reciprocity, mutual care and share, universal love and compassion, fellowship and participation, can offer an effective and more beneficial alternative to the present-day individualistic, materialistic, competitive and consumerist view of life and Reality. There are some seminal ideas, ideals and guiding principles contained here which may help humanity from its present plight. It should be our endeavour to focus on and highlight them taking into consideration the goal of human existence and methods of realizing the same, and thus provide for new social, economic and political order at local and global levels from Jain perspectives.

Jain View of Cosmic Process

One of the most significant implications of the Jain view of Reality is the acceptance that the cosmos, rather the cosmic process, is an organic totality (*samghāta*) of mutually interacting animate and inanimate ontic elements, which though essentially permanent are in constant flux in worldly life and get consecrated as changing events and occurrences. It is exceedingly multifaceted and complicated networking of happenings caused and controlled by karmic forces. It is highly complex and intricate but planned and purposive networking. It is not a mechanistic conglomeration of pre-existent things or entities. In the cosmic process, every existence, living and non-living, has a dependent origin and interdependent existence, a borrowed existence, so to say, out of a causal collocation characterized by mutuality and openness, inter-relatedness and reciprocity. In this empirical world, nothing has self-existence and self-essence as everything arises out of preceding causal factors (*hetus)* and conditions (*pratyayas*). There are no chance happenings or accidents, and no uncaused events or sporadic occurrences. There is a causal concatenation in which there are origin (*utpāda* or *samudaya*) and cessation (*vyaya* or *nirodha*) in an uninterrupted succession till the process comes to complete halt when there is realization of perfection (*mokṣa*). In this causal nexus, every existence has an assigned nature, place and role in the cosmic set-up which can be altered by self-effort. The cosmic process is rooted in ignorance and delusion (*avidyā*) which is a principle of individuation, limitation, circumscription and ego and consequent suffering. It is the root cause, the primal base, the beginning of effectuation.

Uniqueness of Jain Philosophy

Though human thought and value pursuits know no geographical boundaries or barriers, there is something unique and distinctive in each individual culture that needs to be shared at local and trans-geographical spheres. The values posited and pursued in each individual culture are global and universalizable though the way they are posited, pursued and realized is uniquely local to their base. Indian cultural traditions have some distinct and distinguishing features which need to be brought to the fore and highlighted for universal well-being. Just to take the opinion on general Indian philosophy of Charles Moore, Former Professor of East-West Center of Hawaii University, who writes, '*....there are very significant ideas and concepts there–no matter how old they are–to which the rest of the world may well turn for new insights and perhaps deeper wisdom*'. He further writes, '*As said before philosophy is our concern here. But philosophy is not merely an (or the) indispensable medium of understanding and of knowing a people or a culture. Philosophy is also and more basically, of course–the search for knowledge, for truth, for wisdom. In this respect, India provides the basis for a potential philosophical renaissance, if only the rest of the world, especially the West, will search out the new insights, the new intuitions, the new attitudes and methods which might well at least supplement if not replace or correct and at least enlarge the restricted perspective of the Western mind*' [1]. What he says about general Indian philosophy holds good about Jain philosophy as well which is its part.

Symbiosis of Local and Global Thaught

Nature has bestowed upon human being immense potentialities. Systematic thinking is one of the significant ways of utilizing human potentiality in terms of thought constructions and system building with practical orientation and use. Every system of thought is an outcome of felt needs and aspirations of an age and a cultural milieu. Philosophical reflections do not originate in cultural vacuum or in a void. To be meaningful and useful, they have to be rooted in culture-specific experiences. But this does not mean that they do not have universal relevance or utility, as human nature, needs and aspirations are more or less the same. So, philosophy should have at once local and global, individual and universal dimensions. That is why the Indian seers insist that let noble thoughts come to us from all over the world. Human cultural heritage is open to all and should be shared by all. There cannot be any confinement or closed-door approach about it.

Multiple Approaches to Reality

According to Jain viewpoint, Reality is wide, varied and variegated. It is experienced as multifaceted and multilayered. Because it is manifold, there can be multiple ways and approaches to comprehend Reality. The Jain seers emphasized that though in a sense Reality is self-same in its proto-form, both as animate (*jīva*) and inanimate (*ajīva*), in its assumed form it expresses itself in multiple forms and there are multiple ways of expressing our experiences of multifaceted Reality. In view of this rich diversity, there should not be any insistence on uniformity or unanimity in thought that any one particular mode of philosophizing is the only mode of philosophizing or that it alone is logically tenable and sustainable and therefore universally acceptable. So, there cannot be any unanimity or uniformity in our modes of thinking and ways of living. There cannot be any regimentation in this respect. It would be improper and unjust to insist that there can be only one particular mode that has to be universally acceptable. Genuine philosophical activity has to stem from concretely lived experiences that are culturally conditioned, and therefore democracy in ideas has to be the guiding point. There should always be a scope for healthy philosophical disagreement. The thoughtful and creative minds need not always agree or think along a fixed path. There is room for debate and discussion, mutual exchanges, give and take to arrive at truth. This is enjoined in a well-known saying that is preached in philosophical circles, which is '*Vāde vāde jāyate tattvabodhaḥ*' (Truth can be known and realized by mutual discussion and debate.) But this enterprise has to be rational, logical and methodical. Then only, it is reasonable and acceptable. In the past, this viewpoint was properly appreciated and practised and Acharya Haribhadra Suri is best specimen of this, but later on some sort of dogmatism vitiated philosophical atmosphere. There is a need for revival of this approach. Then only, fresh approaches, newer intuitions, novel insights and innovative ideas can be possible.

The point is that none has monopoly over knowledge and truth. It is wrongly regarded that knowledge and truth are confined to and they are exclusive possession of a particular individual or group. Anybody can acquire them. There can be various alternative approaches to Reality, alternative ways to express our experiences of Reality, as also distinct apprehensions of different aspects of the multifaceted Reality. The only insistence should be on systematic thinking and appreciative analysis through monologue, dialogue or polylogue. But this is to be done in the spirit of *samvāda* (concordance of thought) and not of *vivāda* (disputation). A philosophical position has to be logical and rational, but a philosophical disagreement has to be equally logical and rational. The traditional Indian thinkers have gone into details of this modality and have provided voluminous literature as to how *samvāda* is to be conducted avoiding various types of *vivāda*.

As stated above, to agree on some points is philosophical and to disagree on some points is also philosophical. The only requirement is that it should be methodological and reasonable which are the sole guides in philosophical reflections. Of course, in this venture the records of experiences and reflections of ancient seers and sages, saints and thinkers must benefit us but their averments must be banked upon with judicious discrimination. This is *anekāntavāda* of Jainism of which *syādvāda* is a corollary.

Practical Orientation of Jain Philosophy (*Darśana*)

Doing *darśana* is not a brooding arm chair enterprise. It is primarily theoretical and not speculative, and therefore it must have practical overtones. It must entail practice. There is a popular saying that 'knowledge without action is burden'. If philosophical reflection is not applied to concrete life situation, it is incomplete, barren and abortive. It will have an abrupt end if it does not fructify in action in the form of realization. There is no chasm or incompatibility between being and knowing on the one hand and between knowing and doing on the other. The relation among the three is to be viewed as symmetrical and transitive. The Reality is at once all the three, but the modes of their realization are different and varied. This is because Reality is multilayered and multifaceted. This fact is vouchsafed by experience only. We have not to go beyond the ambit of experience to apprehend Reality.

There are several modes of philosophizing available in Indian culture, and among them the Jain mode of philosophizing is most outstanding in terms of its symbiotic nature and most relevant in terms of its utility. It is a thought construction expressible in language to be communicated. If properly understood, Jain philosophy is a systematic reflection upon lived experiences in order to be benefited by the same for realization of quality of worldly life (*abhyudaya*) and ultimately the summum bonum of life (*niḥśreyasa*). It is mainly an enterprise of self-awareness and self-reflection (*Ātmajñāna*) but taking into account the entire gamut of Reality. Right from the dawn of human civilization, Indian mind has been given to philosophical reflections. It has been intuitive and argumentative, descriptive of the nature of Reality and prescriptive of the ideals of life. It has not just been 'love of wisdom' but love for life lived in wisdom, an ideal life, a life worth living. It is essentially goal-oriented, and therefore it is also called *mokṣaśāstra* (emancipating discipline). So, the Jain philosophy begins with philosophy of life, lived and to be lived in this cosmos. It is a search for the ideal of life along with an endeavour to realize the same. It is not mere view of life but a way of life based on it. It has an essential practical orientation. It is basically an activity that is critical and ratiocinative and involves both analysis and synthesis. But this activity is to be undertaken keeping in view the entire wide and variegated Reality that is the object of reflection. By its very nature, it cannot be a piecemeal and compartmentalized thinking even though there can be selective focus on some aspects with some specific objective. It is a holistic enterprise keeping the total Reality in view. According to the Jain point of view, a proper approach to Reality has to be holistic, integral and global in terms of organismic interdependence (*paraspara upagraha*) [2], cooperative partnership (*samgha jīvana*) and supportive mutualism (*sahayoga*) among all the elements (*piṇḍa*) of the totality. This is the implication of *anekāntavāda* and *syādavāda* which are the foundational tenets of Jainism.

Importance of Proper Knowledge (*Samyak Jñāna*)

Jainism is essentially a way of life, but it is a way of life based on a proper view of Reality. Unless there is a correct understanding of the nature of life and Reality through proper attitude and mental make-up (*samyak dṛṣṭi*) and proper knowledge (*samyak jñāna*), there can be no proper mode of living (*samyak cāritra*). *Samyak dṛṣṭi, samyak jñāna* and *samyak cāritra* [3] thus constitute the three jewels which a human being must adorn in one's life. They are therefore known as *triratnas* or *ratnatrayas* [4]. Such a person is known as '*Ratnatrayadhārī*' (possessor of three jewels). Right knowledge (*samyak jñāna*) and right conduct (*samyak cāritra*) are the two foundations of the ethico-spiritual philosophy of Jainism. These two are grounded in right attitude of mind (*samyak dṛṣṭi*).

In Jainism, great emphasis is laid on proper knowledge (*samyak jñāna*). Knowledge is the only and surest way to spiritual perfection. The Jain scriptures therefore emphasize that we must draw a clear distinction between true cognition (*samyak jñāna*) and erroneous cognition (*mithyā jñāna*). Erroneous cognition entangles us in the vicissitudes of worldly life. It is bewitching and bewildering, and it springs from *avidyā* or ignorance. In order to have right knowledge, right attitude or right mental make-up is necessary. This is *samyak dṛṣṭi* [5]. Opposed to this is *mithyā dṛṣṭi* with which we generally suffer. *Samyak dṛṣṭi* leads to *samyak jñāna*, and the latter alone is the path way to *mokṣa*. *Mithyā dṛṣṭi* and *mithyā jñāna* do not serve any genuine purpose, and hence they must be discarded. For an aspirant of *mokṣa/mukti*, only *samyak dṛṣṭi* and *samyak jñāna* are helpful. This is the main theme of the teachings of the scriptures (*Āgamas*). *Samyak jñāna* always leads to *samyak cāritra*. The value and purpose of knowledge is not theoretical but necessarily practical. Right conduct ensues only from right knowledge. As the saying goes, conduct without knowledge is blind and knowledge without conduct is lame. The two are complimentary to each other. And therefore, knowledge has to lead to the corresponding conduct. Without right conduct, deliverance from worldly miseries, trials and tribulations is impossible and without complete deliverance from this no permanent happiness can be achieved. As said earlier, these are the three jewels of life which every human being must wear. But this wearing is not decoration but actual practice and concrete realization. However, this is not easy to achieve. It requires austerity (*tapas*) and *sādhanā*, a rigorous control of body, will and mind. So, knowledge without conduct is useless. Merely listening to the discourses of saints is wastage of time and futile. It does not help us in any way. What is needed is the ensuing conduct. Unfortunately, most of us forget this. We listen to the sermons of the spiritual persons but do not practise them. We take it as a past time or a matter of routine of life. Our knowledge remains mere information at the mental level. The Daśavaikālika sūtra [6] compares a person having knowledge without practice to a donkey who carries burden of sandal wood without knowing its value or utility. As the donkey bears the burden of sandal wood but has no share in the wealth of its load, similarly a person without practice merely bears the burden of his/her knowledge. He/she cannot enjoy spiritual progress which is the real fruit of knowledge. Instead, he/she indulges in evanescent and fleeting worldly pleasures which invariably end up in pain and suffering or mental unhappiness or a feeling of vanity of life. Knowledge is useless without conduct, and conduct is unserviceable without knowledge. In Indian culture, philosophy and religion, view and way, and theory and practice are not divorced and segregated.

Darśana is not mere reflection upon the nature of Reality but also a quest for and realization of values embedded in Reality. There is a definite purpose in life if we care to know and a definite goal to achieve if we have a will to do so. Our existence is not meaningless. It has a value and significance. But we must first of all know what we are, what is the nature and purpose of life, what we should be in our life, how we can be so, etc. The aim of human existence should be spiritual perfection through material progress. But material progress is only a means and not an end. The end is self-realization which is achieved through the removal of *karmic* matter and liberation from *samsāra*. There is potential divinity in human being, and there must be effort for divinization. This is the ultimate teaching of all Jain scriptures (*Āgamas*). We must know the nature of Reality, the *jīva* (living beings) and the *ajīva* (inanimate entities), and also their interrelation. We must know the nature and the role of *karma* and the ways for the cessation of the *karmic* flow which leads to bondage. We must know the distinction between *samvara* (stoppage of inflow of karmas) and *nirjarā* (annihilation of the accumulated *karmas*) along with their respective roles, utility and practice. We must know how and when to practise *caritrācāra* (ethical code) and *dharmavidhi* (spiritual mode of living). We must know the requirements of the practice of a householder and a renunciate. The spiritual progress is a steady and graded realization with gradual purification of soul from decreasing sinfulness to increasing purity, and therefore the theory of *guṇasthānas* [7] (process and stages of self-purification) should also be properly understood so that we may march on this path smoothly and without fail and fall. But all this is not a bookish knowledge which some of us may possess by our readings of the relevant literature, either fully or partly.

Nature of Reality

Knowledge pertains to the real. The real, according to Jain view, has infinite properties (*ananta dharma*), and therefore it can be approached in infinite ways. This is the *anekānta dṛṣṭi* which is the base of *samyak jñāna.* This is Jain perspectivalism at the levels of Reality, thought and language.

The real has three phases of existence. In it, something originates, something endures, and something passes away. So, it is both permanent and changing. But we must know what is permanent and what is changing. We have to attend to both in proper proportion and in proper perspective. More often than not, we do not do so under the spell of ignorance and sway of passion. The *Tīrthankaras*, who are *Jinas (*victors over passions), have shown the way to us which is the right path to be emulated by us. Proper knowledge, proper will and proper effort on our part alone can yield the desired result.

Concepts of *Dravya, Guṇa* and *Paryāya*

The concept of *dravya* (substance) is the crux of the Jain metaphysics. It stands for the totality of things. It is the locus of *guṇas* (attributes) and *paryāyas* (modifications) [8]. The *guṇas* constitute the essential nature of *dravya.* A *dravya* possesses multiple *guṇas. Paryāya* stands for the mode in which a *dravya* and its *guṇas* appear. The most significant and singular contribution of the Jain school in the field of metaphysics is introduction of the concept of *paryāya.* Though the Reality has substantival and adjectival aspects, both substances and attributes exist in a particular form or mode at a particular place and time under particular conditions. This conditioned mode of existence of substance and attributes is known as *paryāya.* The point is that substances and attributes are conceived to exist not in an absolute or isolated way but in relation to other real objects. So, this non-absolutistic or relativistic view of Reality leads the Jain thinkers to postulate *paryāya.*

This rich concept of *paryāya* is a unique contribution which is highly valuable in the spheres of thought and action. It provides a strong base for relativism, perspectivalism and situationalism which are needed for pluralistic worldly life. It helps in avoiding the pitfalls of absolutism, dogmatism, obscurantism, egocentricity and narrowness of all types. It provides foundation to *anekāntavāda* as a theory of Reality and *ahimsā* (non-violence) as a way of life. It alone can ensure a participatory, conciliatory and democratic mode of life which is the aspiration of humankind. Thus, we find that the introduction of the concept of *paryāya* brings about a tremendous modification in the Jain epistemology, metaphysics and value theory, the like of which we do not find in the philosophy of other schools. The implications of this concept are deep and far-reaching in the fields of ethics, logic, mathematics, statistics and linguistic analysis. Its tremendous implications are yet to be brought to the fore by the saints and scholars. Many of such elements have been worked out and developed by the Jain thinkers, but many more are yet to be brought out. For example, the qualitative dimensions of the theory of the probability based on the concept of *paryāya* and theory of karma are unique ideas of Jainism which are only in an embryonic form and if their details are fully worked out, it is sure to result in a Copernican revolution in the methodology of natural and social sciences. It is a challenging task for the scholars of Jainology which should be highlighted and earnestly taken up. This can be achieved if interdisciplinary and multidisciplinary approaches are made to these areas of potential studies and whatever literature exists in this respect is made available in a language intelligible to modern scholars.

Theories of *Naya* and *Saptabhaṅgīnaya*

As stated earlier, according to the Jain thinkers no reality, whether in the form of substance or in the form of attribute, exists as such but only in a specific mode of existence. There are infinite ways or modes in which real can exist, and this idea paves the way for the advocacy of *Anekāntavāda*, the central thesis of Jainism. Likewise, in the field of knowledge, to know a thing is to know its substantial and adjectival aspects in a particular mode or form. A particular mode appears only in a particular set of conditions. With the changed conditions, there will be another mode of existence of that thing. So, all our knowledge of a thing at a particular spatio-temporal locus is conditional and relative to the circumstances. Of course, the possibility of absolute knowledge is all the while there.

As there are many aspects of Reality, there can be multiple approaches to Reality. Each one is true in itself, but it is only partially true. It is true from a particular perspective. From another perspective, it may not be true. We may have a total or holistic perspective, and it is known as *pramāṇa.* But if we have a partial perspective, it is known as *naya.* Both *pramāṇa* and *naya* are true and valuable in their respective spheres. Thus, in the Jain system Reality is cognized in two ways known as *pramāṇa* and *naya. Pramāṇa* stands for knowing the Reality in its wholeness, while *naya* apprehends an aspect of infinitely phased Reality. N*aya* takes into consideration only a fragment of the totality. Of the infinite characteristics of Reality, *naya* pertains to one or a few at one moment. It must be made clear that aggregation of all *nayas* does not constitute *pramāṇa.* It is an independent function of the cognizing mind. Both *pramāṇa* and *naya* are necessary for proper understanding of the nature of Realty. In order to avoid the possible misunderstanding that Reality is exhausted by the acquisition of a particular *naya,* every predication should be preceded by the word *syād* in order to make us aware of the possibility of other alternative predications. This is the doctrine of *syādvāda* which is the logical outcome of *nayavāda.*

Naya has double function. It is experience of object in a particular mode and its verbal expression in that mode. This is the relativistic theory of knowledge and language. Since all partial knowledge is relative, the judgmental and linguistic expression of it has also to contain the relations and the conditions which characterize such knowledge. This is the theory of *syādvāda* [9] which means that every judgment is based on four types of a*pekṣās* (perspectives) of *dravya* (substance), *kśetra* (place), *kāla* (time) and *bhāva* (nature/essence). This theory is further formalized in the form of *sapta-bhaṅgī*, a doctrine of sevenfold predication. It is as follows:

1. From a particular perspective, *it is.*
2. From some perspective, *it is not.*
3. From some perspective, *it is both is and is not.*
4. From some perspective, *it is indescribable.*
5. From some perspective, *it is and yet is indescribable.*
6. From some perspective, *it is not and it is also indescribable.*
7. From some perspective, *it is, is not and is indescribable.*

The last five are permutations and combinations of affirmation and negation.

(1) *Syāt asti* (predication of existence), (2) *Syāt* nāsti (predication of non-existence), (3) *Syāt asti nāsti ca* (successive predication of existence and non-existence), (4) *Syāt avaktavyam* (simultaneous predication of existence and non-predication and therefore indescribable), (5) *Syāt asti avaktavyam* (predication of existence and of indescribability or indescribability as qualified by existence, (6) *Syāt nāsti avaktavyam* (predication of non-existence and indescribability) and (7) *Syāt asti nāsti avaktavyam ca* (predication of existence, non-existence and indescribability).

Professor D.S. Kothari states that *syādvāda* asserts that knowledge of Reality is possible only by denying the absolutistic attitude [10]. *Syādvāda* asserts that a thing is 'A', it is also 'not A', and both 'A and not A', and so on. It is an exhortation to investigate Reality from all different possible viewpoints. It is not a doctrine of indifference or passive acceptance of statements and also their negatives. It is just the contrary. It demands our ascertaining conditions, the coordinate frames as it were, conditions under which it is A or not A, conditions under which it can be both 'A' and 'not A'., and so on. Professor Kothari further opines that the superimposition principle of quantum mechanics provides an illuminating example of *syādvāda* mode of description [10].

Here, it should be clarified that syādvāda is not a system of logic—two-valued or multivalued or fuzzy—in the western sense as it is generally misunderstood and evaluated. It is a theory of expression or speech (*vivakṣā*) and states that each statement is true in its specific universe of discourse. It rejects exclusive particularity of Reality, thought and language.

Anekāntavāda and *Samatva*

The theory of *anekānta*, as stated earlier, is the cornerstone of Jain view of Reality and life. It is described as heart of Jainism. It is a direct corollary of *samatva* (vision of equality), one of the foundational concepts of *śramaṇa* tradition to which Jainism belongs. It is rather application of *samatva*. It is a dynamics of thought which ensures conciliation, concord, harmony and synthesis. It stands for catholicity of outlook and accommodation of different viewpoints in the holistic understanding. It is organismic view of life and Reality. It takes into account both the whole (*sakala*) and the parts (*vikala*). That is why in the field of knowledge it draws a distinction between *pramāṇa* and *naya* to bring home this truth.

Implications of *Anekāntavāda*

The view of *anekānta* is multifaceted comprehending all spheres of thoughts and living. In metaphysics, it calls for non-absolutism and non-dogmatism; in epistemology, it advocates perspectivalism; in logic, it stands for symbiotic approach; in value theory, it appreciates situationalism; in ethics and morality, it puts forth spiritual orientation; in social, political and economic spheres, it advances non-exploitative, compassionate, just and benevolent order; in the employment of science and technology, it cares for sustainable development keeping in view environmental purity and harmony with Nature.

Anekāntavāda as a basic plank of Jain view of Reality and life is the view of manifoldness and multitudinous which provides a basis for peaceful coexistence, corporate living, cooperative enterprises, mutual caring and sharing, judicious utilization of natural and human resources, interconnectedness of all existences and reciprocity. It advocates the sublime ideals of equality, fraternity, justice and non-violence. The Jain philosophy of inclusive pluralism, concomitance, concordance and coordination ensures adaptive flexibility and reconciliation of opposites that is very much needed these days. It is particularly helpful in intercultural dialogues, religious harmony, conflict resolution, social cohesion and peaceful living.

Anekāntavāda, with its corollary of *syādvāda*, provides for democracy in ideas and in living. It inculcates the spirit of tolerance and mutual support. This alone can ensure universal peace, solidarity, friendship and harmony. It is a unique contribution of Jainism which is noble and sublime, deep and subtle. It is not very easy to understand it and to practise it. But if this can be achieved, the world will be an ideal place to live in and to realize spiritual perfection.

Other significant implications of *anekāntavāda* are practice of health care through vegetarianism and environmental protection which are the dire needs of the day. Everything in the world is interrelated and interdependent. Everything has its unique existence and value. So, nothing should be destroyed by the human being for his/her selfish ends. The Jain ethics not only regulates human conduct in relation to one's own self and in relation to other human beings but goes a step further to bring in human conduct in relation to all living beings and natural environment. Every existence has intrinsic worth, and it must be given due respect. In case there happens some misconduct due to ignorance or negligence or even wilfully, there is a provision for forgiveness and repentance. Following the *śramaṇa* tradition, Jainism advocates selfsameness (*samatva*) in all existence in spite of their inherent differences. It thus has the unique feature of synthesizing qualitative monism and quantitative pluralism, monadic uniqueness and modal dependence. In fact, *anekāntavāda* is impregnated with immense possibilities of drawing out newer and newer implications and corollaries for cosmic well-being. But this should not be mere intellectual exercise. It must involve programmatic action at the corporate level on a cosmic scale. This may not be easy but not impossible.

Importance of *Ahimsā*

Understanding of *anekāntavāda* leads to mutual complementarities, mutual cooperation, mutual trust, coexistence and above all to *ahimsā* which is the highest truth and highest virtue in Jainism. *Anekāntavāda* alone can lead to *ahimsā*, and *ahimsā* in turn alone can guarantee peace, progress, prosperity and perfection in the world. *Ahimsā* can also be regarded as extension of *anekāntavāda. Anekānta* is at the level of thought, and *ahimsā* is at the level of practice. The two are thus complimentary. *Ahimsā* enjoins equal respect and mutual dependence of all existences. That is why it is regarded as highest virtue ('*Ahimsā paramo dharmaḥ*'). It is the highest virtue because it alone can lead to spiritual realization.

There are two significant dimensions of *ahimsā*. One is to treat all existences, living as well as non-living *as equal*. This gives rise to a conducive and healthy environmental consciousness. Nature is as valuable as our own existence, and therefore Nature is to be respected. The other dimension is treating all beings as *of equal worth and value*. Therefore, their existence should be preserved and protected. We shall dwell upon these points in subsequent chapters.

Jain Theory of Management

Samatva (equanimity) along with *śama* (self-control) has led to two very important concepts of *asteya* (non-stealing) and *aparigraha* (non-possessiveness). *Asteya* means not to deprive others from their legitimate belongings. Everyone is a part and parcel of this vast universe, and everyone has to have its existence and sustenance in the world. It is the duty and obligation of each one to ensure that the existence and living of everyone is safeguarded and not endangered. We have only to satisfy our legitimate needs and should not cater to our greed. So, the principle of *aparigraha* enjoins to stock only that much which we need. The principles of *asteya* and *aparigraha* guarantee intragenerational and intergenerational justice. Equality and justice go hand in hand. They are the two pillars of Indian theory of management along with two other pillars of *yoga* (supplementing and augmenting existing resources) and *kṣem*a (protecting and not depleting existing resources). These four are the most desirable prerequisites of sustainable development and environmental stewardship.

All social, economic and political organizations are established and aimed at serving human needs and requirements, but they are to be properly managed to serve the purposes for which they are established. For this, the Jain theory of *puruṣārtha* [11] provides broad guiding principles. There are two broad stages of human enterprises. They are production and thereafter distribution and consumption. The guiding principles of production are *kṣema* and *yoga*. *Kṣema* implies use of the resources judiciously so that they are protected for further use and not depleted. Further, usability is natural and their depletion is unnatural. Yoga also implies augmentation of resources and generation of newer and newer resources. This is what should be meant by sustainable development. Environmental stewardship and eco-friendliness are part of this strategy. But real ecology is mental ecology as it is the mind which generates good or perverted human endeavour. A symbiosis of *śama* and *śrama* is called for here. This is professional ethics. It is an efficient management of end, means and modalities in production. After production comes distribution and use. Fair and just distribution and legitimate use or enjoyment both are needed for intragenerational and intergenerational justice. The policy of corporate living, of caring and sharing, implies that we have to care for the present generation as well as for the future generations to come. But ultimately, all human endeavours and enterprises should be a means to and directed towards the realization of cosmic well-being which is the summum bonum of life. It is a state of freedom in which infinitude of the self is restored.

Conclusion

The view of *anekānta* is holistic and integral, comprehending local and global, individual and cosmic spheres. It is therefore necessary to know as to what are its prerequisites and presuppositions, premises and propositions, conclusions and implications. It has tremendous potentiality for a new world order, happy and harmonious, peaceful and prosperous. Delineation on its key concepts, fundamental ideas and seminal practices will help in appreciating the significance of this Jain contribution in the present age of globalization. In this respect, our endeavour should be to dwell upon and highlight Jainism as 'Applied/Engaged Philosophy', a philosophy which is practice-oriented presenting a symbiosis of proper end-means-modality leading to authentic and purposeful living. The main focus should be on sustainable development and judicious consumption which can ensure environmental purity and cosmic order.

As stated earlier, humanity is stationed at a quandary. On the one hand, there are marvels of science and technology, and on the other hand there are value erosions, moral degeneration, and different types of deprivations leading to tensions, strife and suffering. Besides, these problems arising out of globalization are also compelling the ratiocinative human mind to seek for new philosophy of life. The ideas of global ethics and intercultural dialogues unfold themselves in the compassionate, rational and symbiotic Jain ethics of tolerance, interconnectivity and reciprocity and in the basic non-absolutistic postulates which preserve unity and diversity without undermining the identity of either of the two. The philosophy of *aṇuvrata* highlighted by contemporary Jain thinkers Acharya Tulsi and Acharya Mahapragya presents a model of ideal human living. The method of *prekṣā dhyāna* is a practical exercise to mould life according to that model. It is a psychophysical transformation of an individual. On that basis, the art of living known as *jīvana vijñāna* has been developed. Thus, Jain philosophy offers worthwhile perspectives on individual and collective life, social organization, political governance, economic order, globalization and international relations, scientific and technological policies, environmental protection and moral and spiritual progress. It has the capacity and viability for efficacious solutions of global problems. In the following chapters with this background, we shall take some global issues which are threatening not only the very existence of humanity but of the entire galaxy and the cosmos.

Note

Munishri Nyāyavijayaji in the book 'Jain Darśana' (translated in English by Prof. Nagin J Shah) writes, '*None has the right to own exclusively the field of philosophy. Nobody has monopoly on it. Anybody can acquire it. It is wrongly regarded as the exclusive possession of a particular group or sect. When a man respects only that system of philosophy, which he has acquired through family tradition, and dos not cast even a glance at other systems of philosophy, he cannot be regarded as endowed with liberal attitude and catholicity of outlook. Development of knowledge and attainment of truth depend on liberal attitude and wide study.... Truth is not confined to a particular race, class or sect,* etc.' (Introduction, p. XX)

Very perceptively he remarks, '*Though all great men are seekers and cognizers of truth, their search of it and their presentation of it are not identical. The style of presentation, which Buddha adopted, is different from that which Mahāvīra adopted.... It is difficult to get the wholly true knowledge of a thing or reality. Even those who gained it find it difficult to express it in words in its entirety. Their descriptions or presentations of a thing differ from one another or look somewhat conflicting with one another on account of difference of time, place, circumstances, language, style* etc. *This is inevitable*' (pp. XX–XXI).

He further writes, '*Taking into account this situation, Mahāvīra decided to invent such a method that those having incomplete or partial knowledge of Reality or a thing might not suffer injustice at the hands of others. If other's knowledge, though partial and even conflicting with ours, is true, then we should find out such a method that both may get justice. That method is non-one-sided or non-absolutist way or outlook with the wonderful key of this method Mahāvīra, a great saint, unlocked portals of the practical and theoretical problems pertaining to individual and social life.*' (pp. XXI–XXXII), Motilal Banarasidas, Delhi, 1998.

References

1. Charles, M. (2008). *The Indian mind: Essentials of Indian philosophy and culture* (p. 8). Delhi: Motilal Banarsidas.
2. Umāsvāti, A. (2010). *Tattvārthasūtra—parasparopagraho jīvānām*, 5.21. Delhi: Digambar Jain Trilok Shodh Sansthan.
3. Ibid—*samyagdarśanajñānacāritrāṇi mokṣamārgaḥ'*, 1.1.
4. Bhatt, S. R. Jainism in a modern perspective. In: S. C. Prajna & S. K. Samanta (p. 205).
5. Nathmal, T. (1951). *Studies in Jaina philosophy* (pp. 144–49). Varanasi: P. V. Research Institute.
6. Chand, L. K. (Ed.). (1973). *Daśavaikālika Sūtra of Ārya Svayambhava*. Delhi: Motilal Banarsidas.
7. Nathmal, T. (1951). *Studies in Jaina philosophy* (p. 168 ff). Varanasi: P. V. Research Institute.
8. Bhatt. S. R. (Ed.), (2018). *Concept of Paryāya in jain philosophy-introduction* (pp. 5–11). Ahemdabad: L. D. Institute of Indology.
9. Suri, V. D. (1967). *Pramāṇa-Naya-Tattvālokālamkāra* (Chapter-IV, pp. 13–16). Mumbai: Jain Sahitya Vikas Mandal.
10. Kothari. D. S. (1977) *Some thoughts on science and religion* (p. 43). Delhi: Sri Raj Krishna Jaina Charitable Trust.
11. Suri, A. C. (2019). *Puruṣārthasiddhyupāya*. Portland, USA: Generic Publishers.

Suggested Readings

12. Kundakunda, A. (1994). *Samayasāra*. Ajmer: Digambar Jain Samiti.
13. Mahaprajna, A. (2001). *Anekānta: View and issues*. Ladnun: Jain Vishva Bharati Institute Ladnun.
14. Mahaprajna, A. (2002). *Anekānta: The third eye*. Ladnun: Jain Vishva Bharati Institute.
15. Mahaprajna, A. (2000). *Jain Darśana aur Anekānta*. Churu: Adarsha Sahitya Sanga Publication.
16. Mahaprajna, A. (2010). *Anekānta: Philosophy of co-existance*. Ladnun: Jain Vishva Bharati Institute.
17. Mahaprajna, A. (2003). *I and mine*. Ladnun: Jain Vishva Bharati Institute.
18. Tulsi, A. (1996). *The vision of a new society*. Rajasthan: Adarsha Sahitya Sangha.
19. Tulsi, A. (2001). *Bhagavāna Mahāvira: Life and philosophy*. Ladnun: Jain Vishva Bharati Institute.
20. Prajna, C., & Samanta, S. K. (2015). *Jainism in modern perspective*. Rajasthan: Jaina Vishvabharti Institute.
21. Jain, C. R. (1999). *Jainism and world problems*. Bijnor: Jaina Publishing House.
22. Jain, S. (1999). *Multi-dimensional application of Anekāntavāda*. Varanasi: Parshwanath Vidhyapith.
23. Jain, S. (1998). *Jainism in global perspective*. Varanasi: Parshwanath Shodhpith.
24. Kumar, A. (2005). *Jain Darśana Mein Anekāntavāda: Eka Pariśīlana*. Jaipur: Shri Digambara Jain Atisaya Ksetra Mandir.

Chapter 2
Jain Ethics, Environmental Crises and Remedial Measures

Abstract The present chapter deals with a very problematic but highly significant enigma of human life concerning freedom and responsibility in the context of environmental disruption and pollution and consequent ill effects experienced in our concrete day to day living all over the globe due to misuse of freedom and lack of responsibility. The environmental pollution is not just physical in earth, water, air, fire and space. It is at the mental and intellectual levels also. It is all round at the individual level, at the family level, at the community level, at the social organizational level and at the cosmic level. Since all pollution and perversion are human-making, there is need to regulate human conduct. This is real deep ecology. Physical ecology is only external, and it is controlled by internal ecology which is foundational. At present, we only raise environmental concerns and do not care to cultivate environmental consciousness. Instead of trying to treat the outer symptoms, we have to go to the root causes. Then only genuine solution can be brought about.

Keywords *Puruṣārtha* · *Pañcasamavāya* · *Karma* · *Samyak-dṛṣṭi* · Surface ecology · Deep ecology · Economic planning

Introduction

Jain philosophy, of which ethics is a significant ingredient, is a systematic reflection upon lived experiences, both past and present [1]. So, the Jain philosophy begins with philosophy of life, lived and to be lived in this cosmos. It is a quest for the ideals of life along with an endeavour to realize the same. It has an essential practical orientation [2]. That is why consciousness is also characterized as '*upayoga*' [3]. The complex Reality can only be understood by integrating multiple, even seemingly contradictory experiences.

The present chapter is an exercise in self-awareness concerning exercise of freedom and lack of responsibility in the context of the environmental disequilibrium and all-round pollution and consequent disasters experienced in our concrete living all over the globe. These misuse of freedom and lack of responsibility are due to our perverted psyche. It is enigma in the sense that we demand freedom but do not discharge our responsibility coupled with it. We are aware of the prevailing

S. R. Bhatt, *Jainism for a New World Order*,
https://doi.org/10.1007/978-981-33-4041-1_2

disastrous situation and its destructive consequences, voice our concerns and yet we do not make serious and sincere efforts to get rid of it. We do raise environmental concerns at different forums but we do not cultivate environmental consciousness which was imbibed in us by our ancient seers and sages. If we are sincere in this endeavour, we may derive helpful guidance and redemption from the deep insights and enlightening visions of those seers and sages. It has to be a holistic reflection from varied perspectives and multiple approaches. It has to be done with the objective of being benefited by it in shaping the cosmic and human existence for sustainable development and universal well-being [4]. Naturally therefore, the individual human existence, human society, natural environment, scientific and technological enterprises and social, economic and political organizations, etc., become crucial points in a purposeful deliberation. Consideration of deeper issues concerning these areas provides it practical orientation in the context of human life planning, social engineering, science policy and environmental stewardship.

Human Being as Highest Emergent

Human being in the worldly existence is the highest emergent in the cosmic process so far [5]. Shaped by genetic endowment, ecological interaction and cultural transformation, human existence is multi-relational, multidimensional and multi-layered. It has individual, social and cosmic aspects in a holistic and organic framework. It is intimately related to\, other human beings and non-human species. Human identity, therefore, cannot be determined by any one of these facets alone in isolation with others; it is constituted by the totality and intricate unity of all of them [6]. This is proper self-realization.

Human Being as Rational, Free and Responsible Agent

Human being, ideally speaking, is ratiocinative, goal-oriented, free and responsible agent. As a self-conscious and reflective person, he/she has the capacity to understand one's own self as also others. The term used in Indian culture for such a human being is *puruṣa*, and his/her planned, purposive and methodical action is termed as *puruṣārtha.* As ratiocinative knower, human being is endowed with the capacity to know, to discriminate and to form judgement. He/she has freedom of will and can make a choice. He/she is also a responsible agent and has to be accountable for his/her actions. The free will is regulated will. All his/her willful actions should therefore be in the form of *puruṣārtha.* He/she has to perform actions with full knowledge, freedom and responsibility. They should be in the form of '*artha*' (conducive and leading to well-being) and not '*anartha*' (detrimental). Activity is the law of life, and every human being must act as *puruṣa* for survival, sustenance and for enhancement of quality of life. So, there is inclusive alternation between freedom and determinism, free choice and circumstantial limitations. Rationality as discriminative ability implies freedom to choose but being guided by certain norms. It also implies responsibility for the consequences so generated by one's actions. The Jain text Puruṣārthasiddhyupāya and Jain doctrines of '*pañcasamavāya*' and '*karma*' are significant in this respect.

Human Being Responsible for Environmental Pollution

Unfortunately, under the influence of *avidyā* (ignorance/delusion) and false claim to freedom, human mind is prone to perversion and susceptible to wrongdoing and evil. The perversity-prone human mind more often than not indulges in law violation rather than law abidance in this lawful cosmos. This leads to ecological and environmental disruption and pollutions at all levels. Sometimes, this is caused out of ignorance, sometimes by selfishness, sometimes by force of circumstances but more often by weakness of will or perverse habit of mind. It is not unexpected as its seeds are potentially present in human mind because of the past *karmas* which start fructification before one becomes aware of it or makes an attempt to get rid of it. This is one of the facets of the operation of the law of *karma*. This law has attributive facet which needs to be understood properly. It attributes agency to some agent. But it is very difficult to understand this operation and go beyond its labyrinth. Only by right mindset (*samyak-darśana*), right knowledge (*samyak-jñāna*) and good conduct (*samyak-cāritra*), this can be possible.

Significance of Health and Hygiene

Environmental disruption and pollution, imbalance and degradation, are antithesis of health and hygiene. Recognition of value of internal and external health and hygiene, individual, social and cosmic is a hallmark of civilized society. Health and hygiene are essential for socio-economic as also for total development. It is a truism to say that only in a healthy body, healthy mind resides, and when there is psychophysical health, there is spiritual solace. For this, apart from cleanliness of body and external surroundings, purity of eatables and drinkables leading to purity of mind is also necessary along with considerations of quality, quantity and modality of their intake. Health is primarily an individual value (though figuratively we do call 'health of the society or nation'), whereas hygiene is individual, social and cosmic. Maintenance of both health and hygiene is human responsibility for which purity of thought and conduct is essential prerequisite.

Genesis of All Problems

The genesis of all worldly problems is anthropocentric and individualistic attitude of humans. He/she thinks that the cosmos is for his/her purpose and he/she is the master of all and everything exists for his/her sake. He/she is the measure of all and centre of the cosmos. This false understanding breeds greed and selfishness. It is this aberration in thought and practice which is responsible for absence of symbiotic lifestyle in a holistic globe. It is this which generates all conflicts, tensions and disorders. As stated earlier, the problem pervades all levels of existence, individual, social and global. It has become deep rooted. We may wish to overcome it, yet we do not have the required will and the concerted efforts at all levels. We may only hope that saner sense will prevail upon humanity.

Need for Ethics and Morality

Since all perversion and pollution are human-making, there is need to regulate human conduct. There is moral degeneration everywhere. The discipline of ethics is primarily concerned with postulation of norms for good human life and regulation of human conduct in accordance with these norms. On the presumption that human being is a '*puruṣa'* ethical consideration, ethical theorizing and ethical judgements are undertaken. Rationality as discriminative ability implies freedom to choose but being guided by certain norms. The determination and choice of alternatives require norm prescription but human freedom also implies a scope for both norm adherence and norm violation. Values to be pursued and disvalues to be shunned are both equally central to moral considerations. Body, senses, breath and mind are governed by the subtle vibrations (*bhāva*) [7]. The mind, in turn, leads and shapes the entire cosmic process. If we *have kuśala-citta* (righteous mind shaped by *samyak-darśana* and *samyak-jñāna*), we perform good deeds and virtues spread. But if we have *akuśala-citta* (vicious mind), we indulge in bad deeds and vices spread [8]. Delusion (*avidyā*) produces infatuation (*moha)* and dereliction (*pramāda*) which in turn give rise to passions (*kaṣāya*) like greed, hatred and all other vices. Moral degeneration results in pollution within and without. The point to be noted is that no event and no phenomenon, good or bad, is self-existent or eternal. The implication to be derived is that all ecological pollutions have a causal origin, and all these are caused by human mind and resultant harmful actions. Their annihilation also is to be caused by human mind only. This means that both ecological equilibrium and disequilibrium are causal happenings. They are caused by human conduct. As a most evolved species in the cosmos, human has acquired the capacity to preserve Nature or harm Nature. Since we have caused the evils and consequent undesirable suffering, it is our responsibility to eliminate them. This is what can be termed as 'Universal Responsibility'. Since we are the most evolved, we are the most responsible being. We therefore carry a universal responsibility not to create ecological imbalance and to rectify whatever imbalance we have caused because of our folly. As stated earlier, our entire actions stem from our consciousness. If we have pure consciousness (*kuśala-citta*), our actions will be good and conducive to well-being. If we have impure consciousness, our actions will certainly be bad, and they will lead to all miseries and sufferings. Through our actions, we help or harm others and ourselves. All our thoughts, words and deeds are results of our past actions and shape our experiences of the present and the future. What we shall be depend on what we are at present and how we behave in the present. We have therefore to cultivate *samyak-dṛṣṭi* (right attitude) towards life and Reality. We have only to cater to our needs and not to feed our greed. We have become too much selfish, consumerist and exploitative. We have ceased to respect our authentic existence and also the authentic existence of others. Jainism advocates a balanced view of life. Mere material prosperity with the development of science and technology or mere moral and spiritual preaching cannot mitigate worldly sufferings. For a meaningful solution, a symbiosis of the two is needed. Historically right from the times of Tīrthankara Bhagavāna Ṛṣabhadeva, Jainism has been performing this task. Eradication of egocentricity and cultivation of existential openness and universal sameness based on the principles of interdependent existence and interconnectedness of all phenomena enunciated in the Jain tradition are remarkable and the most distinguishing features of Jain ethics that have great relevance and significance in contemporary times and in the new millennium to bring about universal peace, harmony, prosperity and well-being.

Cosmo-Centric Global Eco-Ethics

From the doctrine of interdependent existence of all phenomena, it follows that Jain approach to Reality and hence to ecology is holistic and integral. It does not entertain at the empirical level dichotomy of human–Nature, or Nature–culture, or body–mind, or heredity–environment, or theory–praxis, or thought–action, etc. A holistic approach accommodates differences which may appear to be opposites. Here there is no exclusive 'either-or' but inclusive 'either-or'. There are no rigid structures and no globalized one-size-fits all approach.

Leading an ecologically responsible life is possible by synchronizing five environmental surroundings of an individual—family, community, society, nation and cosmos. The guiding principles for this are *samyakatva* (rightness) and *paras-paraopagraha* (mutual support) [9]. It is an ethical path of enlightened knowledge and conduct. The entire cosmos is a network of mutuality of events characterized by universal interdependence, interpenetration, interconnectedness and interrelationships (*parasparāpekṣā*). In this undivided world, everything miraculously supports everything else. It exhibits mutual interpenetration and interfusion of all phenomena. The point is that there is wholeness of life, self-sameness of all existences, and therefore, we must cultivate universal love, universal compassion, universal kindness and respect for all lives and all existences. Dr. S. M. Jain very pertinently writes, and it is worthwhile to quote him, '*No one constituent in the environment and also no single component or part of any constituent functions in isolation. The boot strap principle of Dr. Geofrey Chew rejects singularity or isolated capability. The manifested properties of any biological or physical unit are there because of the presence and cooperation of others. David Bohm has also authenticated the principle of Undivided Whole. According to Wheeler there is "Quantum Foam" in which every particle is connected with every other particle with quantum interconnectedness. Neither an electron nor any object has any intrinsic properties independent of the environment according to the quantum theory. Every atom in a molecule is important for proper functioning of all other atoms and so are all other atoms for any one atom. In a human body there are trillions of cells and each cell works in cooperation with all other cells for mutual benefit. A single errant cell causes cancer. There are numerous systems and subsystems interlinked and merging into bigger and bigger ones making the composite cosmic whole. An atom is a system and its parts are; electrons, protons and neutrons but parts of a subsystem in a molecule which in turn is a subsystem in a bigger object. Likewise, a living cell is a system for its parts but a subsystem in the organ. A human being is a complete system for its component organs but a subsystem or part in a family, so a family in a society, society in a nation, nation in the world community and entire mankind is part of the biosphere which itself is a part of whole environment, all intertwined, interwoven, interlinked intricately, all incessantly working in mutual cooperation*' [10].

Further, this approach being spiritualistic and teleological from this we get a vision and an approach to cosmo-centric eco-ethics, a widening of moral sensitivity as it views human actions in a cosmic context. In modern times, we need such eco-conduct to solve eco-crises.

Panpsychism

According to Jainism, all natural objects have a spirit residing in them. They are our coinhabitants. As we have a right to live, they also have a right to live. It is therefore a sin to harm or pollute or destroy them. This sort of panpsychism is an outcome of spiritual approach to Reality and life. It also reveals the interconnectedness and interpenetration of all phenomena.

Life of Collectivity

In loving all beings and Nature, there has to be a life of collectivity. The real meaning of life is to be found in the midst of this network of collectivity, a network of interrelationship we call 'life'. Life is to be lived meaningfully in the spirit of cooperation, of mutual give and take, with love, compassion and respect for all. Jain ecology is based on conservation ethics of mutual care and share. Love, compassion and concern for others should be as natural and instinctive as it is for our own selves. It is living with others and living for others and not living on others. There are two very catching and apt words for this idea, i.e. feeling of sameness with others (*parātma-samatā*) and identification of oneself with others (*parātma-parivartana*) [11]. This feeling of oneness is not physical or geographical but mental and psychological. The root cause of suffering is delusion (*avidyā*) and mental afflictions (*rāga-dveṣa*). The consequence of it is feeling of separateness, fragmentation, a sense of separate and independent existence, separated from each other, separated from the environment that sustains us and separated from the things we are inextricably related to. The ecological crises we witness today are the result of this delusion which gives rise to greed, hatred and stupidity.

Engaged Jainism

From Jain teachings, we learn another lesson that ecology is not a mere matter of theorizing or sermonizing but something to be practised. So, all of us have to be 'engaged persons' irrespective of our religious affiliation, whether we are Jain or not in faith. Instead of crying hoarse over environmental pollutions, it is time to act and not to be occupied in discussions and debates or throwing the ball in one another's court. This is important and relevant for us to save this planet from disaster. In this sense, message of Jainism is perennial and eternal. This is enlightenment.

Jain View of Surface Ecology and Deep Ecology

The western ecology is utilitarian, materialistic and mechanical but Jain ecology is spiritual and teleological. In the Jain teachings, we have both surface and deep ecological thinking but their meanings are different than the ones understood by the western thinkers. By deep ecology, the Jain would mean that we have to attend to the functioning of our mind. All good and evil proceed from the mind. Mind occasions our conduct and makes it good or bad. So, we should educate our mind first. This is the foundation of all ecology. This is the real deep ecology that pertains to inner environment. The surface ecology pertains to our actions that constitute outer environment. We feel affected by our actions. They alone are visible and tangible. But they are not basic. They only result from our thinking. Their roots are in our thinking. So *samyak-dṛṣṭi* and *samyak-jñāna* are the basis of *samyak-cāritra*. Knowledge and conduct are two sides of the same coin, but knowledge is more basic. The point is that ecological consciousness is fundamental to ecological conduct. Consciousness operates at the deeper level, and actions are its outward expression at the surface level. Although internal and external aspects can be distinguished, they cannot be separated. They are mutually interdependent.

There is another dimension of Jain deep ecology. Because of its spiritual orientation, it talks of essential unity of all existences. All entities exist in the same form.

All existences have mutuality and participatory being. Actually, there is no 'external other' in ecological considerations. This interconnectedness may not be experienced by deluded empirical mind, and this requires spiritual vision for true understanding of Reality.

Remedial Measures

Having viewed the Jain approach to ecology, we may now discuss the remedial measures. It is to be noted that the problem of environmental pollution is not individual but collective and cosmic, and therefore, the remedial measures also have to be collective and global.

(i) **Respect for Nature**

Human existence, culture and Nature are very intimately correlated. Human being is essentially 'natural' in the sense that he/she is an inalienable part of Nature, is born and brought up in the lap of Nature, is sustained and nourished by Nature and ultimately reaches his/her culmination and consummation in and through Nature. Nature environs human being provides a basis for human evolution as also for excellence and perfection. But in spite of all this, Nature does not exhaust human being; nor does human being exhaust Nature. The laws of Nature condition him/her and he/she can cope up with Nature and with the laws of its operation to some extent. Human being is bound by Nature and yet he/she can transcend the bonds of Nature. He/she is aware of being natural but also of the capacity to overcome and go beyond Nature. Even though dependent upon Nature, he/she can be liberated from Nature with the help of Nature itself. Thus, he/she has a paradoxical awareness of dependence on Nature and possible freedom from Nature. It is a prerogative of human being to acquire this self-awareness and shape his/her life and conduct accordingly.

Nature is lawful and law abiding. Therefore, human being can know and regulate lawful functioning of Nature. But human mind is prone to perversion and susceptible to wrongdoing. It is unfortunate that perversity-prone human mind more often than not indulges in law violation. This is one of the facets of freewill and *karma*. Nature is kind and benevolent. Initially, it gives mild warning, but if no heed is paid it reacts violently. It is left to sweet will of human being to care for Nature and enable Nature to care for him or to be a sufferer of his/her misdeeds.

With a firm base in Nature, human being has the ability to rise above Nature with the help of Nature alone and to become a creator of culture. Both Nature and culture environ human existence and inform his/her being. Both these are distinct but not separate. Both are equally necessary. Culture is humanly transformed Nature. Ideally speaking, Nature should be humanely changed but quite often this turns inhuman. Human existence is a part of Nature, and culture is nurtured Nature but human being tends to make it unnatural. This is the travesty of human rationality and freewill. In an ideal situation Nature, human existence and culture should constitute a continuum or an organic unity but human egotism and selfishness come in the way.

It is to be highlighted that Nature has its intrinsic value as well as instrumental worth. We have forgotten the intrinsic value of Nature and have taken it as merely instrumental. We forget that we are products of Nature since we are embodied self and we are sustained by Nature. Instead, we try to conquer Nature and try to have mastery over it. This is our ignorance, our *mithyā-dṛṣṭi* (wrong view). Indian sages and seers always respected and loved Nature and wanted to be in the lap of Nature. The guiding principle is if we care for Nature, Nature will care for us. If we destroy Nature, Nature will destroy us. This is the simple principle of interdependence. So, it is saner to preserve and protect Nature, rather worship Nature as a spiritual entity. Nature is beautiful and bountiful. It is full of joy, and it gives joy to us. It is joyful and joy-yielding. Let us appreciate and preserve this quality of Nature. Nature is to be approached with respect and gratitude. A life in the lap of Nature is a mark of spiritual freedom. It is freedom from all restraints, physical and mental. It is widening, deepening and heightening of spirit. It is a life of purity, internal and external. Life in Nature is natural life. We should ideally lead a life of a 'green person' caring for Nature and sharing the bounties of Nature. To repeat, if we care for Nature, Nature will care for us. If we pollute Nature, it adversely affects our existence. Nature is an 'Embodied Love' and 'Embodied Benevolence'. For example, trees do not exist for themselves, they stand in the sun and provide shadow not to themselves, and they yield fruits and other benefits not for themselves. They do so for the sake of others. The same is the case with rivers, mountains and other objects of Nature. In this respect, Nature is a great master and a teacher practising and teaching *maitrī* (loving kindness), *karuṇā* (compassion), *muditā* (sympathetic joy), *upekṣā* (equanimity), *kṣamā* (forgiveness), *sahiṣṇutā* (tolerance) and *samatva* (selfsameness).

(ii) **Doctrine of Ahimsā as a Guide to Ecology**

As stated earlier, the physical and external pollution is due to mental and internal pollution. It is due to *mithyā-dṛṣṭi* and *akuśala-citta.* This moral degradation affects the individual as well as his or her surroundings. The remedy lies in recovering the lost vision of wholeness and practising *ahimsā.* The need is to establish a *vratī samāja* (virtuous and righteous society).

The doctrine of *ahimsā* provides a foundation to an environmental perspective to be offered to humanity to meet the present-day crises that are endangering and threatening all existences human as well as non-human. It also helps in bringing about an ecological lifestyle. Ecological thinking and ecological living go hand in hand and a symbiosis of the two has been the keynote of the Jain view and way of life. Concern for the well-being of the living beings and the physical world has been an important element throughout the history of Jainism. Human existence and destiny are inextricably linked with environments. Recognition that human beings are essentially dependent upon and interconnected with their environments has given rise to instinctive respect and care for all living beings and Nature. Every existence from elementary particles to plants, animals, birds and human is participatory members of the planetary community having personal dignity, inherent worth and inviolable rights to exist and grow.

Ahimsā is not just non-killing but a positive action in the form of unselfish friendliness and compassion for all existences based on the spirit that all existence is as sacred as our own existence. It therefore preserves life and ensures durable peace. *Ahimsā* further implies giving due opportunities to all existences for self-preservation and self-development. There should be no deprivation or exploitation. *Ahimsā* also means removal of suffering of others, offering joy to them, service to all needy and active involvement for good of all. Love, compassion, kindness, friendliness and concern for others should be as natural and instinctive as it is for our own selves. It is an enlightened view and way of life.

Apart from loving Nature, the Jain tradition has always advocated love and respect for all beings. All living beings are creatures of Nature. Nature provides them from physical form and sustains them. Nature environs them and provides them nourishment. So, the principle of *ahimsā* tells us that one which you want to kill is your own self as your existence depends on that thing [12]. So, earth, water, air, fire and space all have life to be respected and preserved. In order to ensure firm faith in this belief, a living tree is associated with all Tīrthankaras and insistence in the lap of Nature is highlighted. The insignia of all Tīrthankars are also living beings. The theories of nine nidhis and fourteen ratnas have similar ecological considerations [13].

There is another reason for respecting the life of all living beings. Jainism has advocated the doctrine of cycle of birth and rebirth. This implies kinship with all creatures. We may take rebirth as any of such creatures depending upon our *karmas*. These creatures could have been our parents or sons or daughters in their previous births. So, to kill some being is to kill one's own relative. Therefore, vegetarianism is the safest practice to escape from this eventuality. Vegetarianism is good for healthy living also.

(iii) **Doctrines of *Aparigraha* and *Samyam* as Guiding Principles of Eco-ethics**

One of the three facets of *Śramaṇa* tradition is *śama*. It means *samyam* which stands for limitations of wants, desires and possessions (*parigraha-parimāṇa and icchā-parimāṇa*), curb on unlimited cravings, unlimited accumulation and unlimited consumption. Acquisition of wealth is not bad, only attachment to it or its misuse is to be avoided. The guiding principle is 'Use that which is needful and give the surplus for charity'. The doctrine of *aparigraha* advocates limited use of natural resources, non-violence and vegetarianism. There has to be sustainable production and fair distribution. Everyone has equal right to share the natural resources, and therefore, there should be no deprivation.

Thus, *aparigraha* stands for non-consumerist attitude wherein the policy is, there should be production only if needed and not first production and then arousal of needs as is the practice these days. The present-day policy of advertisement, allurement and seduction should be stopped. True renunciation is a state of mind of a human being. It is not only renunciation of unnecessary material goods or consumerist mindset but also evil thoughts and feelings (*kaṣāyas*), rigid attitudes and wrong beliefs. Carelessness, selfishness, obstinacy and greed are the causes of violence. Their eradication requires cultivation of pious mind by *dhyāna* and practice of virtuous conduct by observation of vows, particularly of giving up something in the form of self-restraint. Six positive virtues (*śukla leṣyās*) help in preservation of physical and mental ecology. The twelve precepts enumerated in Uvasagadāsao [14] are directly or indirectly connected with environment. In fact, all *Mahāvratas, Aṇuvratas, Guṇavratas* and *Śikṣāvratas* are foundational to Jain view of ecology and are related to *ahimsā* and *aparigraha.*

(iv) New Paradigm of Economic Order

Apart from individual and social moral disciplines referred to above, we have to attend to world economic order which is closely related to and dependent upon the environment. The ignorance or failure of modern economic theory to acknowledge this fact has resulted in multiple ills and evils in the world. It has become a threat to the very system which has created it. The growth attained under this model is unsustainable. This apart, it has made human self-centred, greedy, insensitive and violent. What is needed is a radical paradigm shift in economic planning and execution in the form of 'Relative Economics', 'Regenerative Economics' and 'Compassionate Economics'. The details of this will be discussed subsequently as a separate chapter.

(v) Need for Cosmic Vision

The vision of self-sameness of all existences and zealous longing for eradication of sufferings of other's as one's own cross all barriers of race, creed, country and even humanity. The benevolent teachings of universal compassion and cosmic goodwill, living and working for totality all these have a significant message for the present-day distracted humankind suffering from exhaustion of spirit and languishing in the narrow and rigid confinements of ego-centrism, parochialism and disastrous materialistic consumerism. There is a dire need for a total transformation of our values, ideals, beliefs and attitudes. A time has come for the beginning of a cultural renaissance for which the Jain teachings can play a vital and pivotal role. Jainism has come into existence as a problem-solving exercise both in terms of prevention and of cure. The Jain teachings are of great relevance and significance in contemporary times and in the new millennium to bring about universal peace, prosperity and well-being. These should be our guiding lights for our ecological thinking and doings. On account of lack of restraints, selfishness and proneness to feed greed rather than catering to the needs, there has been all-round pollution of environment at all levels—physical, mental, emotional and intellectual. In modern times, we are voicing concerns only for physical environment without paying due attention to other types with the result that not much headway is made even in protecting the physical. There cannot be divisive and lopsided approach to environment. Even at the physical level, all the *pañcabhūtas*, viz. earth, water, fire, air and space, are to be taken care of. Environmental stewardship implies a sense of mutual care to be spearheaded by human beings only.

These and related issues may be taken up for threadbare analysis by scholars working on environmentalism. But apart from theorizing, practical concerns must be paramount. Knowledge without action is futile. In the Indian tradition, it has been emphasized that right knowledge (*samyak-jñāna*) has to fructify in right conduct (*samyak-cāritra*). In Jainism, great emphasis is laid on proper knowledge (*samyak-jñāna*). Knowledge is the only and surest way to spiritual perfection. Proper knowledge can be imparted only by proper education.

(vi) **Role of Education**

Education is a conscious, deliberate and planned process of modification in the natural growth and development of human being and the surroundings. If proper and adequate, it ensures accelerated processes of development in human life in right rhythm. It is therefore a means for betterment and enhancement of quality of life. It is useful for personality development, character building and for livelihood. It is a hall mark of civil society. But all this becomes utopia if it is not properly conceived and implemented. As Prof. Muni Mahendrakumar has rightly stated, '*Ultimately, education should teach man how to lead a really happy, healthy and peaceful life free from conflicts and violence, and infused with the spirit of love and altruism, leading to peaceful co-existence*' [15]. If we have to draw eco-syllabus for eco-education, it has to be on Jain foundation to be meaningful, efficacious and practical.

Conclusion

While concluding, it should be reminded that human being is at the climax of cosmic process. He/she possesses vast potentials for betterment or devastation. He/she can be a superbeing or supermalignancy. He/she has a choice and also the capacity of judicious discrimination. Since he/she is the most evolved, he/she should be the most responsible. He/she has not only to voice environmental concern but also to cultivate environmental consciousness. Mere sermons and seminars will not help. Unless the overall physical and social environment is congenial and symbiotic, nothing will improve substantially. For this, we need environment-friendly value system and a suitable code of conduct. There has to be inner moral conviction and a moral attitude. We have to induce ecological age and ecological mind. Through proper education alone, this is possible.

References

1. (a) "*I wish philosophers should not adhere simply to the explanations given by the predecessors but develop some new theories by which far from being stagnant philosophy can prove to be a progressive mentor for ushering in a new world.*" Samani Chaitanya Prajna and Samari Kanta Samanta, (Ed) 'Jainism in Modern Perspective', Foreword by Late Acharya Mahaprajna, Jain

Vishwa Bharati Institute, 2015, Ladnun. (b) "*But, however Jain philosophy needs to be redefined and refined to better fit into a highly anarchical world order marked by new challenges and myriad conflicts*" (Prof. B.M. Jain) Ibid., p. 53.

2. Jain, S. (1998). The solution of world problems from Jain perspective. In: S. Jain & S. Pandey (Ed.), *Jainism in a global perspective* (p. 142ff). Varanasi: Parshvanatha Vidyapitha.
3. Here 'upayoga (Uvaoga)' means cognitive function which is the defining characteristic of soul.
4. (a) Dasavealiyaṁ 4.8—*Jayaṁ care jayaṁ ciṭṭhe jayamāse jayaṁ sae/Jayaṁ bhunjanto bhāsanto pāvaṁ kammaṁ na bandhaī//* Here the word 'Jayaṁ' means self-restraint and care and caution in conduct; its opposite is *pramāda* (carelessness). For care and caution the mendicant is supposed to have knowledge of entire gamut of Reality as said in the same text—*jo jīve vi viyāṇāī, ajīve vi viyāṇaī/ jīvājīve viyāṇanto, so hu nāhii sanjamaṁ//* (4.13). (Ed.) Acharya Mahapragya, Ladnun, Jain Vishwa Bharati, 3rd ed., Ladnun, 2007. (b) Dasavealiyam verse 7.2. (Ed.) Acharya Mahapragya, Ladnun, Jain Vishwa Bharati, 3rd ed., Ladnun, 2007.
5. Cf. *Pañcasamavāyas* of Jainism (see Jain Darshan–Munishri Nyāyavijayaji, Eng tr. Nagin J Shah, p. XXIII., Motilal Banarasidass, Delhi, 1998.
6. Prajna, S. C. (2015). Anekanta: A new paradigm of philosohy of co-existence and non-absolutism. In S. C. Prajna & S. K. Samanta (Eds.), *Jainism in modern perspective* (p. 15ff). Ladnun: Jain Vishwa Bharati Institute.
7. Acharya Mahapragya in "Amantrana Arogya ko", English translation by Prof. S.R. Bhatt under the title "Invitation to Health", pp 172ff., Adarsh Sahitya Sangh, New Delhi, 2013.
8. Āyāro, 2.48 Quoted in Sagar Jain-Vidya Bharati, vol. I, p. 143.
9. (Tattavārtha Sūtra. 5.17–22).
10. In Jainism in Modern Perspective "Role of Jainism in evolving a Global ethics", pp. 52ff.
11. (a) *Tumasi nama sacceva jam hantatvam ti mannasi,* Ayaro,5.10. (b) *Sattveṣu maîtri guṇiṣu pramodam, kliśteṣu jīveṣu kṛpāparatvam. Madhyasthabhāvam viparītavṛtau sadā mamātmā vidadhātu deva.* (Prayer).
12. (a) Trees associated with Tirthankaras–Sagar Jain-Vidya Bharati, Vol. I. pp. 141–2. (b) Insignia of Tirthakaras are animals (Ibid., p. 142). This is eco-theology.
13. Ibid., p. 143.
14. Ibid., 144.
15. The Role of Jainism in Evolving New Paradigm of Philosophy. In S. C. Prajna & S. K. Samanta (Eds.), Jainism in modern perspective (pp. 3ff). Foreword by Acharya Mahaprajna, Jain Vishwa Bharati Institute, Ladnun, 2015.

Suggested Readings

16. Rankin, A. (2018). Jainism and environmental philosophy: Karma and the web of life. Routledge, London.
17. Prajna, C., & Samanta, S. K. (2015). Jainism in modern perspective. Ladnun: Jaina Vishva Bharati Institute.
18. Chapple, C. (2002). *Jainism & ecology—Nonviolence in this web of life*. Harvard: Harvard University Press.
19. Chapple, C. (2006). *Jainism and ecology*. Delhi: Motilal Banarsdas s.
20. Chapple, C. (2001). *The living Cosmos of Jainism: A traditional science grounded in environmental ethics*. California: Loyola Marymount University.
21. Kothari, D. S. (1977). *Some thoughts on science and religion*. Delhi: Shri Raj Krishen Jaina Charitable Trust.
22. Jain, C. R. (1999). *Jainism and world problems*. Bijnor: Jaina Publishing House.
23. Reading, M. (2019). *The Anuvrat movement: A case study of Jain-inspired ethical and eco-conscious living*. Switzerland: MDPI Journal.

24. Shah, P. (2009). *Jainism—Religion of compassion and ecology*. California: Jain Education Committee.
25. Sogani, K. C. (2001). *Ethical doctrines in Jainism*. Solapur: Jain Sanskriti Samrakshak Sangh.
26. Tatia, N. (1951). *Studies in Jaina Philosophy*. Varanasi: P.V Research Institute.
27. Trelinski, B. (2010). *Deep ecology and Jainism: A critical assessment of theory and practice*. Canada: Queens University.
28. Tucker, M. E. (2018). *Routledge handbook of religion and ecology*. London: Routledge.

Chapter 3
Ahimsā as Overriding Principle of Jain Ethos

Abstract The principle of *ahimsā* is a distinguishing feature of Indian cultural ethos. In Jainism, it is advocated in a most rigorous form. It is regarded as a foundation of all other virtues. In the present turbulent world, its necessity is felt all over the globe. The UNO celebrates 2 October as 'Ahimsā Day' after the birthday of the apostle of *ahimsā*, Mahatma Gandhi. Under his Guru Shrimad Rajachandra, Gandhi was highly influenced by the teachings of Jain philosophy. This evinces its importance. In this chapter, this concept is discussed threadbare in relation to all other virtues and it points out its necessity in contemporary times.

Keywords *Ahimsā* · *Dharma* · Truth · Equality · Peace · Friendship · Justice · Ecology · Conflict-resolution

Introduction

One of the most distinguishing features of Indian culture is its advocacy of *ahimsā* (non-violence) as supreme virtue for right modes of thinking and harmonious ways of living. Among all the virtues, it is regarded as the highest and most fundamental (*Ahimsā paramo dharmaḥ*'). It is a dharma in all its three facets of being *dhāraka* (sustaining principle), *niyāmaka* (regulating principle) and *sādhaka* (life-enhancing principle) of all existences. The principle of *ahimsā* has been an integral part of Indian cultural ethos. Since India's remotest past, it has been reiterated time and again by great seers and sages and enlightened people each one adding a specific flavour to it. In the multi-hued tapestry of Indian culture, the principle of *ahimsā* shines as the most foundational principle, and all cultural traditions have accepted it as a basic tenet. In Indian culture, *ahimsā* is not a creed or dogma but an article of faith, a way of life and an item of living practice. It stands for a mental make-up of respecting all life and existences, protecting and caring for them and enhancing their nature.

S. R. Bhatt, *Jainism for a New World Order*,
https://doi.org/10.1007/978-981-33-4041-1_3

Need for *Ahimsā*

At present, we find that all over the world, there is disproportionate and unbalanced increase of material progress inconsistent with spiritual enhancement. Rise of egoistic tendency and selfishness, greed and cutthroat competition, deprivation and exploitation, adulteration and consumerism, environmental pollution and spread of diseases and disasters, terrorism and violence, conflicts and wars, etc., all these have made our life miserable. There is no happiness, peace and contentment. All the five material elements, viz. earth, water, air, fire and space, all psychical elements, viz. mind, intellect, heart and consciousness, all spheres of the universe, viz. inner space, intermediate space, super space and super most space, all social, economic, political and international organizations, etc., have been vitiated, and their basic nature has been violated. The averment of Vedic systems of '*trividham tāpam*' (threefold suffering) and famous saying of the Buddha, '*Sarvam duhkham*', (All phenomena are misery mongering) have been symbolic expression of this plight. There is violence to one's own self, to fellow beings, to Nature and the cosmos. Of course, one has not to be pessimistic about all these as all these happenings are caused by human being, and human being can eliminate them given right mode of thinking and harmonious ways of living. In this age of tremendous rise of science and technology and their wonderful achievements as also outbursts of religiosity, there are terrible dangers due to perverted mentality almost universally prevalent which is vitiating the global atmosphere and therefore there is need of ahimsā more than ever before. Prof. D.S. Kothari opines very pertinently that '*Ours may be called an age of science, but it is certainly not a scientific age. It is not an age of reason or rationality, not yet. That can only come when science and ahimsā equally find a place in man's thoughts and actions.*' [1]. We are living in an era of dreadful dangers, and the only remedy seems to be the practice of *ahimsā* in all its forms and facets. As a law of life, it alone is the surest means to peace, progress and plenitude, material prosperity and spiritual enhancement.

Causes of Violence

The root cause of violence is infatuation caused by ignorance and delusion. It is mental. It gives rise to passion and mental perversion. Hatred, anger, enmity and antagonism give rise to violence. This apart, fear and lack of strength also cause violence. Among many other reasons, one of the dominant reasons is material progress disproportionate to spiritual enhancement. This has resulted in all ills and evils. Everywhere injustice and deprivement leading to tension, hatred, jealousy, violence, murders, killings and wars are rampant. Though people want peace and happiness, these are eluding our grasp. There is perversion and unchecked selfishness due to crass anthropo-centrism and materialistic outlook. We are not in peace with others and not in peace with ourselves also, and there is discontentment. The whole society everywhere is in turmoil. But there is no need to be pessimistic. There are remedial measures which we must learn and use. The Jain culture has put forth several such measures, among which *ahimsā* is the uppermost.

Ahimsā in Jainism

Among all the cultural traditions of India, Jainism has put forth practice of *ahimsā* topmost. No doubt all accept *ahimsā* as supreme virtue but in practice Jainism outdoes all. It can be said without exaggeration that *ahimsā* is the very essence of Jainism. According to Prof. K. C. Sogani, *ahimsā* can incontrovertibly be called the beginning and the end of Jain religion. He states that in the view of Samantabhadra, it is the paramount principle of Jainism. The whole of Jain *ācāra* (code of conduct) is a derivation of this principle. On the basis of Ācārāṇga, he writes that *ahimsā* is pure and eternal dharma. It is a dharma itself, but it protects all other dharmas [2].

Jainism as a part of *śramaṇa* tradition of Indian culture pivots round the principle of *ahimsā* in all derivations of the word '*śramaṇa*' as *sama, śama* and *śrama.* It inculcates the spirit of equality and equanimity (*sama*), freeing people from selfishness and attachment, having moderation and uprightness in thought, words and conduct leading to self-control and benevolence (*śama*) and caring and working for intragenerational and intergenerational justice through virtuous conduct (*śrama*). These alone can guarantee individual progress, social harmony, economic prosperity, political stability and above all global peace.

Nature of *Ahimsā*

Though the word '*ahimsā*' is negative in its coinage and grammatical formulation, its meaning and connotation are deeply positive. It stands for peace, friendship, amity, compassion and coexistence with cooperation in all spheres of life. On the contrary, '*himsā*' (violence) is negative as it amounts to threatening or destruction of life and existence. *Himsā* is defined as taking away life out of passion ("*Pramattayogāt prāṇavyaparopaṇam*") [3]. It is willful determination to harm life. Negation of *himsā* is *ahimsā*. *Ahimsā* is negative of the negative and hence positive. It turns minus into plus and returns peace and happiness. It opens favourable opportunities, creates conducive conditions and enables us to achieve the proximate and ultimate goals of life. It elicits love and friendship and inculcates positive attitude. It is basically a positive mental attitude. It is natural essence of all life and existence. On the contrary, *himsā* is not natural. It is caused by extraneous factors. It breeds hatred, generates enmity, results in loss of life and gives rise to all sorts of negative results. The Puruṣārthasiddhyupāya of Amṛtacandra [4] states that the emergence of any sort of passion in the self is *himsā*. The self in its pure form is *ahimsā*. Speaking from the transcendental point of view, even the slightest fall or deviation from complete self-realization is *himsā*.

Ahimsā Is Integral and Comprehensive

In Jainism, there is integral approach to *ahimsā*. It is both internal and external. It is at once mental, verbal and functional. It comprehends individual life, family life, community life, social life and cosmic life. It brings in its fold living and non-living existences. It touches all places and all situations. Among all these, internal is basic. *Samatā* (equanimity) is inner aspect of *ahimsā*. It stands for calmness, tranquility and serenity of mind without which there cannot be peace within and external social harmony, world peace and cosmic wellness. This not only brings about spiritual contentment, illumination and bliss in one's self, one's consciousness or life force and its supporting elements like body, senses, mind and intellect but also in the supporting systems like family, society, state and the world. We may call it as spiritual non-violence and spiritual regeneration.

Ahimsā Is Instinctive and Intrinsic

All living beings seek pleasure and avoid pain. All want self-preservation and self-enhancement. (*Savve pānā jīviu kāmā*). Everyone wants to live and live happily. So, any act to thwart or hinder this natural tendency amounts to violence. This is built in the nature of all existences, and therefore, it is the fundamental principle of orderly cosmic process. Cosmos has life-sustaining elements in abundance. Any attempt to disturb or misuse them is violence. It is our universal responsibility to preserve and enhance these elements. *Ahimsā* is also intrinsically valuable. It is the very nature of all existences. It is desirable for its own sake. It is an end in itself. Everything else follows it or is from it. It opens up new avenues for peace, progress and plenitude.

Ahimsā Is Indivisible

The Jain thinkers counsel that, 'do not insult, abuse, oppress, enslave, injure torment, torture or kill any living being'. Lord Mahāvira says that '*You are that which you intend to hit, injure, insult, torment, enslave or kill*'. He further says that '*One who neglects or disregards the existence of earth, water, air, fire and vegetation, disregards his own existence which is entwined with them*' [5].

Tumamsi nāma sacceva jam hantatvam iti mannasi,
Tumamsi nāma sacceva jam ajjāveyavvam iti mannasi,
Tumamsi nāma sacceva jam paritāveyavvam iti mannasi,

Tumasi nāma sacceva jam parighetavvam iti mannasi,
Tumamsi nāma sacceva jam uddaveyavvam iti mannasi.
(One who you think should be hit is none else but you.
One who you think should be governed is none else but you.
One who you think should be tortured is none else but you.
One who you think should be enslaved is none else but you
One who you think should be killed is none else but you.)

There is a very catchy Sanskrit term '*ātmaupamya*' which means that all entities are equal and therefore all are like one's own self. This obliterates the distinction between self and not-self and results in compassion and fearlessness. Every creature loves one's own life. No one wants to be harmed or killed. Everyone wants to live fearlessly, smoothly, safely and happily. Therefore, no creature should be killed (*Savve pānā na hantavvā*). By doing violence, not only the victim is affected but all those who depend upon that victim. So, it has wider percolation.

Ahimsā and Service (*Sevā*) to Others

Jain texts like Ācārāṇga dwell in detail about the importance of service to others. This follows from the principle of interdependence. One should serve others selflessly and with humility. This implies sacrifice of one's own narrow interests for the sake of others. Social harmony and cosmic well-being are possible only if coexistence is coupled with cooperation and mutual care and share.

Ahimsā Is not Cowardice

It is not easy to practise *ahimsā*. It requires self-control and courage. On the contrary, only coward resorts to *himsā*. One commits *himsā* out of fear. *Ahimsā* makes one strong and fearless. It is not to submit to the will of evil doer. Rather it entails the will and courage to fight evil for the welfare of society. However, while fighting, one should have the feeling of love and sympathy for the evil doer. 'Hate the sin and not the sinner', so the saying goes. So *himsā* is necessary for self-defence and for general welfare. But this is only in exceptional cases, and this requires judicious discrimination. Mahatma Gandhi borrowed this idea from Jainism and practised it.

Himsā Is Sin

To do violence, to make someone to do so, or to approve or permit someone to do so, is sinful. To deprive someone from genuine mode of living is also sin. Life, in whatever form it is, should be respected and protected. We have no right to take other's life, because everyone wants to live as we want to live, and nobody wants to die.

Types of *Himsā*

Ahimsā like peace is indivisible and all comprehensive. But there can be some exception to it. This is because all worldly existences are relative to time, place and circumstances, and there can be no rigidity in this. In the Jain literature, four types of *himsā* are classified. They are as follows:

1. *Ārambhi* (unavoidable)—Even after being careful, there is unavoidable *himsā* in daily routine work.
2. *Udyogi* (occupational)—For essential professions like agriculture and in some industries, violence may not be avoidable. So, for the sake of ultimate good violence is permitted.
3. *Virodhaja* (protective)—When someone is attacked by enemy or violent creature, reciprocatory violence is permitted. This is for the purpose of self-defence only.
4. *Samklapika* (deliberate)—This is willful and intentional violence which should not be condoned in any way. It is this which is condemned and prohibited.

Other important types of classification of *himsā* are internal and external, within and without. It is intrapersonal and interpersonal. It is to one's own self and to others. It is material and spiritual. It is further classified in terms of *dravyahimsā* and *bhāvahimsā.* Pruṣārthasiddhiyupaya asserts, '*One who has not abandoned the mindset of himsā commits himsā even though he may not actually indulge in himsā. Thus, wherever there is inadvertence of mind, body or speech himsā is inevitable*' [6]. So, basically it is mental and all else are its manifestations.

Ahimsā and Cognate or Allied Terms

Ahimsā is closely related to all virtues which become its cognate or allied terms. Some of them can be enumerated as truth, love, compassion, friendship, fellowship, sacrifice, mutual care, welfare, development, peace, harmony, trust, austerity, self-restraint, health care, fearlessness, etc. In the Praśnavyākaraṇasūtra [7], non-violence is equated with sixty virtuous qualities. Thus, it represents all virtues.

Ahimsā and *Anekānta*

Ahimsā is a resultant phenomenon of *anekānta* and is safeguarded by *anekānta.* *Ahimsā* and *anekanta* are mutually reinforcing. To admit that the real is multifaceted implies that there can be diverse approaches to Reality and each one is true in itself. This generates mutual tolerance and respect.

Ahimsā and Law of *Karma*

Himsā and *ahimsā* are both actions and therefore abide by the operation of the law of *karma*. Performance of *himsā* causes bondage and sufferings, and adherence to *ahimsā* earns happiness and merits. Jain ethical code exhorts to cultivate *samyakcāritra* (virtues conduct) on the basis of *samyakjñāna* (right knowledge). One who performs virtuous deeds earns merits and contributes to the wellness of the society. Good deeds are to be appreciated, and bad ones are to be condemned and punished.

Ahimsā and Truth

Ahimsā and truth are inseparable. Truth provides theoretical foundation, and *Ahimsā* is its practical counterpart. Truth (*samyakatva*) has been given great importance in Jain tradition. Truth stands for non-deviation. Truth in moral context is steadfast adherence to virtue [8]. A truthful life consists in mutual caring and sharing. It is a life of interdependence and reciprocity.

Ahimsā and Equality

Ahimsā is the same as treating all entities as equal or as having intrinsic worth and value. All beings are equal, and life in every creature should be respected. All living beings desire to live and desire a long and happy life. They detest sorrow and death. Everyone has the right to exist, and no one has any right to kill or harm others. The principle of non-violence embraces not only humans, birds and animals but also trees, vegetables, air and water as all these are considered as living beings with souls. As such, they also feel pain when injured or destroyed. So instead of following the principle of 'Living on others', we have to follow the principles of 'Living with others' and 'Living for others'. This is the implication of the maxim '*Parasparopagrahojīvānām*' given in the Tattvārthasūtra [9]. There cannot be social harmony and progress without mutual cooperation. *Ahimsā* embraces the universal law of love and compassion for all which is an indispensable requirement for the smooth existence of family, society, nation and the world. It is the willingness to sacrifice one's narrow interest for the sake of others, a sort of merging our own will into the wills of others. It is true and unconditional surrender of our own identity for the welfare of others. So, once *ahimsā* is assimilated, it manifests itself in equal treatment of all living beings and even inanimate objects. This is possible only through self-conquest.

Ahimsā and Happiness

Observance of *ahimsā* brings about joy. It is joyful to help and not to harm. It gives unique satisfaction to preserve, protect and enhance life (*yoga-kṣema*) of a living creature. This can be done for the sake of earning merits as people generally do, but it can be for joy's sake also as we share the same spirit and coexistence with all creatures. We want to live and enjoy and so do they. Further, it is joyful to be in the lap of Nature, and therefore, we should help Nature to make us joyful. This can be done by plantation or protecting vegetation. In India, we have the tradition of celebrating '*vanamahotsava*', to go and live in Nature and to experience immense joy. We also have the convention of maintaining '*pañcavaṭi*' by growing such trees which give shadow and oxygen. Not only seers and sages lived in forests, we also aspire to be there at least for some time for the sake of enjoyment.

Ahimsā and Peace

Ahimsā and peace are two sides of the same coin. The two are intimately corelated. There cannot be peace in the absence of *ahimsā. Ahimsā* alone generates peace. Further, there cannot be peace without welfare. The welfarism propounded in Indian thought is not materialistic welfarism but holistic welfarism. It is spiritualistic welfarism that envelops but also transcends material well-being in which the welfare of not only the individual but the whole humanity and the entire cosmos is taken into consideration. The well-known prayer '*Let everyone be happy. Let everyone be without hunger and disease. Let everyone experience the good and the noble and let no one meet with suffering.*' is a hallmark of *ahimsā* in practice.

Peace and Sustainable Development

Peace and sustainable development also go together. The term 'sustainable development' is a fashionable catchy word these days, and it has acquired popular currency for socio-economic developmental policies and strategies with a concern for quality of life, intergenerational and intragenerational justice, preservation of ecosystems, forestry, natural capital, etc. The traditional Indian perspective of development represented by the terms 'svasti', 'śivam', 'kalyāṇa', 'maṇgala', etc., meaning universal well-being has been genuinely sustainable by virtue of being holistic, integrated, all comprehensive and futuristic taking into account individual, social and cosmic dimensions of existence in its material as well as spiritual aspects. It envisages no incompatibility or antagonism or conflict among these, as they are all conceived and experienced as interrelated and interdependent elements of one and the same whole.

Right from the dawn of human civilization, India has always projected the sublime ideal of cosmic unity and universal perfection. Projecting the inspiring ideal of the entire cosmos being one family (*vasudhaiva kuṭumbakam*), the Indian culture has tried to inculcate the attitude of seeing self-sameness everywhere (*sarvatra sama dṛṣṭi*) and of being engaged in the well-being of all existence (*loka samgraha*) without any selfish consideration (niṣkāma *bhāva*). Hatred and malice towards none, friendliness and compassion for all, absence of deprivation and exploitation in all respects, this has been the quintessence of Indian culture at all times in all traditions. The famous '*Śāntipāṭha*' of Indian culture sums up the Indian vision of sustainable development or total development as follows:

Aum dyauḥ śāntirantarikṣa śāntiḥ pṛthivī śāntirāpaḥ śāntirauṣadhayaḥ śāntiḥ vanaspatayaḥ śāntiḥrviśvedevāḥ śāntiḥrbrahma śāntiḥ sarva śāntiḥ śāntiḥreva śāntiḥ sā mā śāntiredhi.

(May there be peace and prosperity in the outer space and inner space, on earth, in the waters, in the life-giving vegetable kingdom, in plants and trees, in the entire cosmos, in the entire Reality, everywhere and at all times. May there be peace and prosperity, Peace and prosperity alone (never otherwise). May everyone attain and experience peace and prosperity.)

In the history of humankind, the need for peace has never been as acute as it is today. The reason is that there has been all-round animosity and such a dangerous increase of weapons of mass destruction that the entire human race can be eliminated. War first starts in the human mind, and not elsewhere, due to perverted psyche. Further, our lopsided materialistic approach to development has resulted today in multiplication of disparity and deprivation, injustices and imbalances, subjugation and inequalities leading to disruption of peace. There has been all-round moral degeneration resulting in alarming rise in crime and corruption. There is no denying of the fact that during nineteenth and twentieth centuries, there has been rapid and tremendous progress in science, technology and in all walks of material life. But the fruits of all this progress have not only been inequitably distributed but they have also been counterproductive and evanescent. Never there have been such disasters and destructions threatening annihilation of life and existence. Even in a traditional country like India, there has been a steep decline and collapse of value system under the impact of this materialistic onslaught upsetting the geographical and social ecology. The way pollution is increasing and the rate at which crimes and criminals are mushrooming make us doubt as to whether it is a development sustainable and worthwhile.

Ahimsā and Friendship

Ahimsā and friendship are closely correlated. It is looking at others with tenderness and compassion. This friendship is for all existences, living and non-living. Generally, we have friendship with other human beings and sometimes with animals or birds and other living creatures, but it has to be extended to Nature as well. Friendship is expressed through love and care. One who has love for all beings will have no enmity with anyone. He who takes delight in harmless living and sharing love with all will have enmity with none. This loving kindness is the basis of peaceful coexistence, smooth cooperation and just mutuality. This should be the guiding principles for good life.

Ahimsā and Conflict Resolution

Ahimsā is the antidote of conflict. It is the practice of *anekānta.* Some people like Huntington talk of clash of civilizations. Of course, this has been a fact of history, but this cannot be regarded as desirable. Instead, we should talk and work for harmony of civilizations. Now is an era of cultural pluralism and global interdependence. So, there cannot be ethnic seclusion or cultural imperialism. Truth cannot be monopolized by any single individual, community, race or religion. Contradictions may be there, and there can be differences of opinion. These are unavoidable but they need to be reconciled. Reconciliation is natural and desirable. There should be dialogues and polylogues, exchanges of ideas and views.

Ahimsā and Harming Others

Some perverted mind may seek pleasure in revenge, in harming others. Teasing, pulling down, rap or any such evil act may appear to give pleasure to the agent, but it is not only sadistic, it vitiates one's psyche and results in evil consequences. It may appear to give momentary pleasure but ultimately it results in suffering. It is not natural happiness which springs from within. *Himsā* inflicts pain on the victim resulting in fear or loss of life, etc., but it also causes pain internally on the person who does *himsā.* Therefore, the happiness of an individual can only be ensured by working for the happiness of others.

Ahimsā and Forgiveness

Ahimsā is intimately connected with forgiveness. In the worldly life knowingly or unknowingly, there is always a possibility of doing violence or hurting someone, some organism living in air, water or on earth. For this, the Jain tradition highlights the role of seeking forgiveness. For this purpose, a specific function is held every year. It is known as *Kṣamāvāṇīparva* or *Paryuṣana* or *Dasalakṣaṇaparva* or *Samvatsarīparva.* While observing this function, it is stated that we should beg pardon and forgiveness for all intentional or unintentional wrongs, excesses, sins done to any being. There is celebrated verse for this atonement which is employed for this purpose. It is as follows:

> '*Khamemi savve jīvā save jīvā khamantu me*
> *Miti me sarvabhuteṣu veram majjham na kanae*' [10]
> (I forgive all living beings, may all living beings forgive me.
> I am friendly to all living beings; I have no animosity towards any living being.)

This is a significant ceremony of self-reflection and self-purification. It involves the act of *pratikramaṇa* which means to look or turn back to recollect if any harmful thought or action happened last year so that there can be begging of forgiveness. This act of repentance and confession is a mental, emotional and spiritual process of ceasing to feel resentment, indignation, anger or hatred towards another person for perceived offence or mistake or harm and not to undertake or demand retaliation or retribution or punishment. It is a significant expression of non-violence. The process of shading the effects of our *karmas* really begins by asking for forgiveness with genuine feeling and with a vow not to repeat mistakes. The quality of forgiveness is humility and suppression of ego and anger. To grant forgiveness, one has to first get over anger, pride and ego. Then only genuine forgiveness is possible towards person who has harmed you. Similarly, to ask for forgiveness from the person whom you have harmed, you must first subdue your own ego, resentment and hatred towards that person prior to asking for forgiveness from him. Forgiveness is a very powerful instrument to win over someone. There is a popular saying that forgiveness is the embellishment of brave (*Kṣamā vīrasya bhūṣaṇam*). And it helps us to be better human beings. It is a harbinger of social harmony, concord and amity also apart from self-purification leading to *mokṣa*. It puts in practice the exemplary principle of 'Live and let live'.

Ahimsā and Health Care

Ahimsā and health are also correlated. Health is not negation of disease. It is a positive state. Taking medicine, curing disease and restoring health, this is not the right understanding of health. In such situation, again there will be disease and loss of health. Again, medicine will be taken and then health will be restored. In this way, health becomes a handmaid of medicine. This is not the proper way. Health is rather a positive feeling. It is mental strength, creative thinking, pure memory and pure consciousness. It is our natural capacity. By this, we are always at ease and not dis-eased. By implication, it means that health is our disease–deterrent capacity. The sounder is the health, the stronger is the human. Negative thinking and negative feeling both diminish disease–deterrent capacity. Unbridled play of senses weakens the power of preventing disease. Medicine is to be administered to one who invites ailments. The treatments of negative attitude and of unbridled play of senses imply invitation to health. Conversely also, positive attitude and control of senses mean invitation to health. The root cause of all suffering is false understanding of the nature of Reality, existence and life (*mithyā dṛṣṭi*). So, Jainism emphasizes the need to realize right knowledge (*prajñā*). This is possible only by proper mode of living (*śīla*), and this in turn requires meditative practice (*dhyāna* and *samādhi*).

It is much easy to invite disease. But it is very difficult to invite health. Everyone desires to be healthy both mentally and physically. Then only one can be happy and contented. Health of mind and health of body are interrelated. Both are the desirable goals of a balanced life. In the present age of strife and environmental disharmony, health has become a coveted goal. Prevention is better than cure. So, it is needed that we prevent the possible occurrence of disease. Very often we suffer from physical and mental ailments. For physical ailment, we go to a doctor for cure. But for mental ailments, only cultivation of a positive mind is helpful. For this, we go to spiritual Gurus or psychotherapist and seek their advice. This can be done by personal interaction with them or by reading their books. Only through right knowledge and meditation, this can be removed. So, meditation is medication.

Ahimsā and Vegetarianism

Vegetarianism is a necessary manifestation of *ahimsā*. It is simply a logical extension of the habit of looking upon other living beings with love and compassion. For maintenance of health, both mental and physical, vegetarianism is necessary. Reverence for life, as a foundation of *ahimsā*, results in strict observance of vegetarianism and veganism. In Jainism, there is a great emphasis on respecting life and protecting life. In currently available eatables, vegetarian food is the best and par excellence, and this was accepted thousands of years ago.

Food is an important means of fulfilment of the will to live a healthy life of hundred years. The best food for human being is that which is helpful in keeping him/her away from mental and physical illness and from extraneousness harmful influences and also in making a healthy mind and a healthy body. Healthy body is due to healthy mind and vice versa. In healthy body, positive emotions are generated. Pure food has tremendously significant role in giving rise to healthy mind free from rashness and impulsiveness and in generating healthy emotions and healthy body. Therefore, it is evident that the basis of human excellence is vegetarianism.

The philosophy of *ahimsā* (non-violence) is very subtle. One has to enter into the depth of this philosophy in order to understand the differential balance between violence to vegetation involved in vegetarianism and violence to living beings necessarily involved in meat eating. This requires a judicious distinction between the two forms of violence.

Ahimsā and Ecology

The central theme of *Ahimsā* not only means that one should not create a situation in which any living being is harmed or killed but it also means that one should not create circumstances which disturb inanimate order. So *ahimsā* relates both to animate and inanimate existences. There is reciprocal interdependence between the two. This interdependence is the gift of Nature which must be valued. Nothing exists by itself. The physical environment is conditioned by the living beings, and the living beings in turn are conditioned by physical environment. The two have to coexist. *Ahimsā* and environmental purity are intimately correlated. If the environment is polluted, it will have direct effect on life-sustaining energy which we derive from Nature. This in turn will affect our mind and soul. So, *ahimsā* is not just confined to non-killing but extends to preservation of Nature also. Both physical and mental ecology are to be kept pure and free from pollution. Mental ecology is more fundamental, and therefore, Jainism pays more emphasis on that. We have already discussed this in the earlier chapter. Here we reiterate it for the sake of emphasis. *Ahimsā* is the most important means for human and non-human well-being. Protection of physical environment and biodiversity is necessary for human survival and progress. Survival of Nature is our own survival. Every existence in the universe is sacred and has intrinsic worth and instrumental value. So, it must not be harmed or thwarted. For this, we have to control our needs and wants. One has to be *icchājayī* (victor of desires). It is necessary that we appreciate the value of self-restraint.

Ahimsā and *Aparigraha*

The practice of *ahimsā* demands observance of non-possessiveness (*aparigraha*). It stands for curbing of desires and taking that much only which is necessary for existence. There should be no boundless greed, uncontrolled desires. One has to set limit to personal acquisition, wants and unnecessary consumption. These imply caring for intragenerational and intergenerational justice. *Aparigraha* also means that to deprive others from their legitimate needs is theft and deceit.

Ahimsā and Economic Policy

While pursuing economic enterprises which are necessary for worldly living, purity of means is always to be kept in mind. As the saying goes, 'Honesty is the best policy'. In all activities of production, distribution and consumption, moral values have to be the uppermost. There should be no erosion of moral values of any sort. There should be no selfishness or cruelty or exploitation of human or animals or use of insecticides in production and preservation of food items. There should be no bonded labour or excessive labour with less remuneration, no depriving in distribution, and no excessive or hedonistic pleasure in consumption. It has to be economics of social service, of fulfilling needs, of eradicating poverty. Profit should not be the motto, and utility and service should be the guiding principles. It should be economics of mercy and compassion. There should be no adulteration. In production, harmful or dangerous items should not be manufactured. This apart from environmental protection, absence of pollution, care for purity of Nature and judicious use of natural resources, etc., should be kept in mind. In other words, business ethics should be the overriding and controlling principle.

Three Guiding Principles of *Ahimsā*

Ahimsā is not just to be theorized but to be put to practice by human being in judicious manner. It is a harmonious way of life. For this, the guiding principles are as follows:

1. *Sahavāsa* (coexistence). It stands for corporate living (*samgha jīvana*) in a *vṛiti samāja* (virtuous society)
2. *Sahakāra* (cooperation) and
3. *Sahabhoga* (mutual care and share)

All the three together may be comprehended under '*parasparopagraha*' (mutual support).

Remedial Measures

The remedial measures for elimination of *himsā* and realization of *ahimsā* are as follows:

1. Adherence to *pañcamahāvratas* of *ahimsā, satya, asteya, aparigraha* and *brahmacarya.*
2. Be messengers of global peace and non-violence as they are to be realized universally.
3. Form *ahimsā* brigade to disseminate awareness about it.
4. Practise eradication of *kaṣāya* (defiling vices), curb greed and selfish cravings, curtail wants (*icchāparimāṇa*) and adhere to a*steya* and *aparigraha.*
5. Education can play a vital role in spreading the message of *ahimsā* to the most impressionable young minds.

Since violence or non-violence is basically a mental attitude, one has to be constantly vigilant, careful and considerate. In Jain literature, we find mention of virtuous and evil qualities, and we are advised to refrain from evil ones. The root cause of evil qualities is delusion. This leads to the feeling of separateness, of attachment to one's own self. We feel that we are independent existence. We lose the vision of wholeness. Hence, there is need for right education. To conclude, we state the ancient maxim, 'Rise, be awakened and do not stop till the goal is achieved'.

References

1. *Some thoughts on science and religion* (p. 9). Delhi: Sri Raj Krishna Jaina Charitable Trust (1977).
2. *Ethical doctrines in Jainism* (pp 41–42). Jaina Sholapur: Samskriti Samrakshaka Sangh (1967).
3. Umasvati. (1993). 'Tattvārthasūtra' 7.8 (Ed.) Pt. Sukhlal Samghavi, Prashvanatha Vidyaypitha, Varanasi.
4. Amrtacanda, 'Puruṣārthasiddhyupāya' 45–48. Central Jain Publishing house, Lucknow, 1933.
5. Ibid., 45–48.
6. Ibid., 45–48.
7. Jain, S. (1994). 'Sagar Jain Bharati', Pt. 1, Parshvanatha Shodhapitha, Varanasi, p. 18.
8. 'Samaṇa suttam', verse 96 states as follows: *Saccammi vasadi tavō Saccammi sañjamō taha vasē sēsā vi guṇa. Saccam ṇibamdhṇam hi ya guṇāṇamudadhīva macchāṇam.* (Truthfulness is the abode of penance, of self-control and of all other virtues; indeed, truthfulness is the place of origination of all other noble qualities as ocean is that of fishes.)
9. 'Tattvārtha sūtra', 7.8.
10. Generally recited in the ceremony.

Suggested Readings

11. Mahapragya, A., & Gandhi, S. L. (Eds.). (2009). *Training in non-violence-theory and practice.* Jaipure: Anuvrat Global Organisation.
12. Mahaprajna, A. (2005). Anekānta, Ahimsā aur Śānti. Delhi: Adarsha Sahitya Sangha.
13. Mahaprajna, A. (1994). *Astitva aur Ahimsā.* Ladnun: Jain Vishva Bharati.
14. Mahaprajna, A. (2008). Yugin Samasyā aur Ahimsā. Delhi: Adarsha Sahitya Sangha.
15. Acarya, T. (2013). *Religion, Anuvrat and human wellness.* Delhi: Adarsha Sahitya Sangha.
16. Acharya, T. (1996). *The vision of a new society.* Sardarsahar: Adarsha Sahitya Sangha.
17. Tulsi, A. (1950). *Jaina Siddhānta Dīpikā.* Sardarsahar: Adarsh Sahitya Sangh.
18. Jain, J. P. (1944). *Religion and culture of the Jains.* Delhi: Bharatiya Jnanpitha.
19. Jain, S. (1988). *Jainism in global perspective.* Varanasi: Parshvanath Shodhpitha.
20. Jain, S., & Pandey, P. (2002). *Ahimsā kī Prāsangigatā.* Varanasi: Parshvanatha Vidyapitha.
21. Jain, K. (2018). *The applied philosophy of Jainism.* Varanasi: Parshvanath Vidyapeeth.
22. Jaini, P. (1979). *The Jaina path of purification.* Delhi: Motilal Banarsidass.
23. John, K. (1990). *Roots of conflicts, conflicts resolution through non-violence.* Delhi: Concept Publishing Company.
24. Kothari, D. S. (1977). *Some thoughts on science and religion.* Delhi: Shri Raj Krishen Jaina Charitable Trust.
25. Lane Diem, A. (2016). *Ahimsā: A brief guide to Jainism.* California: Mount San Antonio College.
26. Geeta, Mehta, & Kokila, Shah. (2012). *Various fascets of Samana Suttam.* Mumbai-Delhi: Somaiya Publications.
27. Nagin, J. S. (1996). *Jaina theory of multiple facets of reality and truth.* Delhi: Motilal Banarasidass.
28. Ramjee, S. (1992). *Jain perspective in philosophy and religion.* Varanasi: Parshvanath Shodhpitha.

29. Sims Lana, E. (2016). *Jainism and nonviolence: From Mahavira to modern times*. Ohio: Cleveland State University.
30. Sethia, T. (2004). *Ahimsā, Anekānta and Jainism*. Delhi: Motilal Banarasidass.
31. Sogani, K. C. (2001). *Ethical doctrines in Jainism*. Solapur: Jain Sanskriti Samrakshak Sangh.
32. Stevenson, S. (1970). *The heart of Jainism*. Delhi: Munshiram Manoharlal.
33. Tatia, N. (1971). *Jainology and Ahimsā*. Vaishali: Vaishali Institute Research.
34. Tatia, N. (1951). *Studies in Jaina philosophy*. Varanasi: P.V. Research Institute.

Chapter 4
Aparigraha—As a Mode of Balanced Life

Abstract One of the most disturbing phenomena is prevalence of economic disparity among individuals and nations. As a consequence, poverty and hunger are the two evils affecting individual life and social harmony. A few persons and nations have amassed huge wealth and have control over means of production and development. Others who are deprived of this live in abject poverty. The stratification between rich and poor has been responsible for domination of a few over vast majority. The rich who have accumulated enormous wealth control global economy. The rich want to be richer and usurp as much as they can to control market. The device of globalization, which is material, has been invented by them for profiteering and to have full sway all over the world. The instinct of possessiveness blinds their vision. They become mad after wealth which becomes an ultimate goal and end of their life. This gives rise to competition and conflicts, discrimination and deprivation, monopolistic and overpowering tendency. As opposed to this, seers and saints have exhorted people to get rid of this perverted mentality and to ensure justice and fairness. But all their exhortations have proved futile. In Indian culture, this reckless pursuit of wealth is regarded as evil and sinful. The Jain thinkers have been quite vocal about this. What is needed is new lifestyle of simplicity and mutual caring and sharing.

Keywords Aparigraha · Need · Greed · Possessiveness · Non-attachment · Charity

Introduction

Aparigraha (non-possessiveness) is the most important principle of Jain ethics and for that matter of entire Indian ethics, which, if adhered to sincerely, can usher in an era of lasting peace and happiness. It is a part of '*Pañcayāma*' or '*Pañca Mahāvrata*', five mandatory vows prescribed in Indian culture. It is a valuable ideal not very easy to practise but this does not minimize its worth. Jain seers, particularly the Digambaras, do practise it to the fullest extant. Ideals are not utopian dreams. They are prescribed to be pursued and practised. But this requires a proper mindset cultivated through proper education and discipline (*sādhanā*).

Some Jain thinkers regard *aparigraha* more basic than *ahimsā*. Following Acharya Tulsi, Acharya Mahapragya often said that instead of '*Ahimsā paramodharmaḥ*' we

S. R. Bhatt, *Jainism for a New World Order*,
https://doi.org/10.1007/978-981-33-4041-1_4

should say, '*Aparigraho paramodharmaḥ*' [1]. He regards non-possessiveness as the highest virtue, higher than non-violence. This is because possessiveness gives rise to violence, and therefore, it is more basic and rudimentary. It is the main cause of violence and precedes it. Non-violence cannot be appreciated without first realizing non-possessiveness. Violence and possessiveness go together. In fact, the two are complimentary. The only graceful way to escape reactive violence is to willingly put a limit on possessiveness. The natural consequence of this discipline will be an equitable distribution of goods.

Possessiveness means excessive passions and consequent attachment to objects, both internal and external. These result in all problems faced by humanity. So *aparigraha* (non-possessiveness) is the need of our age. In today's world, it has become as important as non-violence. Unlimited desires and accumulation of wealth lead to possessiveness and storage. Possessiveness gives rise to the mentality of consumerism also. This results in exploitation, discrimination and deprivation because rich people usurp and hoard most of the products and deprive poor people from their legitimate use. To eradicate the ill effects of consumerism limitations of wants is needed [2].

Definition of *Aparigraha*

Aparigraha is defined as '*Savvāao bahiddhādānāo veramaṇam*' [3]. In this definition, *bahiddhā* means external, *ādāna* means acceptance, and *veramaṇam* means abstinence. So *bahiddhādānāo* means acquisition of and attachment to external objects; and *bahiddhādānāo veramaṇam* means abstinence from all kinds of possessions, both internal and external. This is *aparigraha.* In Tattvārthasūtra (7.12), Umāsvāti defines *parigraha* as *murcchā,* insatiable desire. It is clinging to objects, animate and inanimate [4]. The two definitions express the same fact representing the practice of '*śama*'.

Causes of Possessiveness

The root cause of all worldly problems is ignorance or false knowledge about one's self and the external world. The self has to be detached from objects of the world. Under ignorance, the self develops desire to possess objects and identifies oneself with them. The self then gets entangled with the objects of the world. This gives rise to false ego, the mentality of 'I', 'me' 'mine', etc.; and also, divisive outlook of 'I' and 'thou', 'mine' and 'yours', etc. The self regards objects as his own exclusive possession and not of others. The result is the vicious circle of desire and aversion, usurpation and hoarding. Excessive passions and unrestrained desires cause perversity of human nature. Desires have no end. They are limitless. To satisfy them, one may resort to all means, fair or foul. Possessiveness is vice. It is a great hindrance in virtuous living. For spiritual practice, it is the first thing to be avoided.

Basically, *parigraha* arises from within. The evil tendencies give rise to perverted human psyche. They generate vices which are termed as internal enemies. Six cardinal vices have been enumerated as *kāma* (lust), *krodha* (anger), *lobha* (greed), *moha* (delusion), *mada* (pride) and *mātsarya* (jealousy). They are called *granthis* (knots which bind or tie). Since Jainism insists on their eradication, it is called *Niggantha dhamma*. One who overcomes these vices is regarded as *mahāvīra*, great victor. One who is completely free from all possessiveness is clam, tranquil and serene in his/her mind and experiences bliss.

Consequences of Possessiveness

Owing to attachment, a person commits violence, tells lies, commits theft, indulges in wrong sex and resorts to unlimited hoarding and consumerism. Possessiveness leads to fear, tension, frustration and anxiety. It is the root cause of suffering. It has not only given rise to greed and infatuation but also competition and conflicts. This has affected social harmony because of economic disparity. Further, it has caused environmental disequilibrium and pollution. Therefore, excessive accumulation of things is a sin. It is a crime against Nature and humanity.

Remedy

All problems of the world are human-made. Natural calamities are also due to human folly. Human is free to perform good deeds or bad deeds. Instead of doing good things, more often he/she indulges in evil deeds. The vices make him/her prone to evil. In fact, we have to be realist, pragmatic and worldly wise. We have to conquer our own self. Mastery over our self by our selves is supreme virtue. We have to fight with our own narrow self. Self-control and self-restraint are the pathways to peace and happiness. Conquering external foes is not the right way to get peace and happiness. For this, restraining senses and subduing mind are necessary. The practice of self-control is compared with controlling a horse with reins. Knowledge, meditation and penance are the reins. They can bring about extermination and extinction of attachment and control greed.

Need and Greed

The earth has plenty of resources. There is no shortage of resources to sustain us. So, there is no need to hoard. Mahatma Gandhi averred that the mother earth has enough for everyone's needs but not for everyone's greed. But the perverted human being overlooks this fact. He/she should limit wants and possessions but on the contrary he/she accumulates whatever he/she can. If this perverted mentality is checked and eradicated, then there will be no hunger and poverty.

There are some articles of daily life which are required for worldly existence. But they should be used only to fulfil the basic needs of life. They are to be resorted to meet only bare necessities of life. Any attachment to them gives rise to vices. The basic discipline is to limit quantity of things one will use. For this, self-imposed restriction is required in terms of limiting personal possessions (*Icchāparimāṇa*) and avoiding wasteful expenditure. A disciplined person leads simple life without compromising legitimate personal needs.

Charity and Philonthrophy

Another aspect of non-possessiveness is charity and social welfare with the feeling of mutual cooperation, care and share. This involves least minimization of one's own needs and giving the rest as donation and gifts to the deserving and needy ones. Its negative aspect is non-acceptance of gifts if this is motivated for allurement or seeking favour. Abstinence from accepting of gifts is refusal to appropriate them or be influenced by them.

Benefits of *aparigraha*

The mindset of non-possessiveness has many benefits. It ensures economic equality and justice. Then everyone will be able to fulfil one's needs. There will be no deprivation leading to violence, jealousy, hatred, theft, dacoity, etc. There will be no class conflict.

Another good consequence will be absence of consumer culture. There will be no hoarding and misuse or wasteful expenditure. Rich people and nations have so much of wealth that they do not know how to utilize it. They indulge in consumerism and encourage consumerism for their selfish ends. There are many evil effects of consumerism. For this, *aparigraha* is the only remedy.

Non-possessiveness helps in maintaining ecological equilibrium. Unnecessary and wasteful production puts a burden on Nature. Natural resources are not inexhaustible, and therefore, they should be used sparingly and judiciously. Present economic, scientific and industrial policies are resulting in non-sustainable development. Exploitation of Nature in the form of damaging and degrading the shrinking resources has not augured well for human welfare. The so-called Industrial Revolution has been harmful and counterproductive as well. Therefore, we have to evolve a new value structure based on scientific knowledge and logical thinking. At present, there is total chaos and anarchy in the field of values. There is valuelessness prevailing all around. We have understood human being as struggling and fighting animal forgetting the divinity inherent in him/her. The animal instinct lying within us is dominating our psyche. Though we talk of higher spiritual values, in our behaviour we are controlled by devilish forces. Because of materialistic and mechanical outlook, we have lost sight of spiritual values. The result is tension everywhere. We have lost peace and happiness. We have to take wealth as a means for universal welfare and not as an end.

In the Jain social organization, a distinction is drawn between a renunciate and a householder. Extreme form of renunciation is practised by a renunciate. In the Digambar sect of Jainism, a renunciate does not possess anything, not even clothes to cover the body. He practises extreme form of self-restraint and austerities. Of course, this is not prescribed for the householder who is required to follow a middle path. This is the ideal that the world has to emulate. Possessiveness is vice. It is a great hindrance in virtuous living. For spiritual practice, it is the first thing to be avoided.

For intragenerational and intergenerational justice, the ideal of *aprigraha* is not only desirable but also necessary. This alone can ensure global peace and prosperity. For this, proper mindset through right type of education and training in control of mind and senses is needed. In the history of mankind, there have been many examples of great souls who have rigorously followed this precept. It is not difficult to amulate them, given the will and determination. Mahatma Gandhi under the influence of Jainism practised this lifestyle.

References

1. Mahapragya, A. (1994). *Astitva aur Ahimsā* (p. 59). Ladnun: Jain Vishva Bharati.
2. Tulsi, A. (2001). *Bhagwan Mahavira: life and philosophy.* Ladnun: Jain Vishva Bharati.
3. Thāṇam. (1984). Caujjāma-padam, 4.1.136. Y. Mahapragya (Ed.), Ladnun: Jain Vishva Bharati.

Suggested Readings

4. Mahaprajna, A. (Ed.). (1994). *Ācāro Bhāṣyam.* Ladnun: Jain Vishva Bharati.
5. Jain, K. (1983) The concept of Pañcaśīla in Indian thought. Varanasi: P.V. Research Institute.
6. Jain, K. (2018). *The applied philosophy of Jainism.* Varanasi: Parshwanath Vidyapeeth.
7. Sogani, K. C. (2001). *Ethical doctrines in Jainism.* Solapur: Jain Sanskriti Samrakshak Sangh.
8. Tatia, N. (1951). *Studies in Jaina philosophy.* Varanasi: P.V. Research Institute.

Chapter 5
Vegetarianism: A Preferred Diet

Abstract The contemporary lifestyle has given rise to several such problems by which the whole humanity is under severe strain. Now it is being realized that without changing the lifestyle, it is difficult to get rid of those problems. The most important constituent of lifestyle is food or diet. It has been commonly accepted that those who have a lifestyle dominated by non-vegetarian food compared to them the life of vegetarians is healthier. A lifestyle of taking beneficial and small quantity of pure food is preventive and curative means of many problems of health, and this has been proved by eminent medical scientists and nutritionists. Medical science has declared non-vegetarianism to be the greatest culprit for the rise of many dangerous physical diseases like cancer but this apart even in the context of emotional health it is made known in psychology that meat eating is dominant cause in the increase of wicked emotions and infatuations. Those who know the principles of ecology and environmental science maintain that definitely non-vegetarianism is very dangerous to human as it pollutes Nature and cause illness. The usefulness of vegetarianism in comparison with non-vegetarianism can be proved on the basis of spirituality, religion and philosophy along with physiology, psychology, sociology, ecology and other branches of modern sciences. By echoing the voice of peaceful coexistence as 'Live and let live', this chapter pleads for vegetarianism to live pure, healthy and inexpensive life and to give up non-vegetarianism and liberate the self.

Keywords Vegetarianism · Biopotential · Vital energy · Human body · Healthy diet · Fasting · Science of nutrition

Introduction

As stated earlier in the chapter on *ahimsā*, the spring of life is vital energy and energy comes from food. Much depends upon how human takes material particles from outside as food. The best food for human being is that which is helpful in keeping him/her away from mental and physical illness, from extraneous harmful influences, and also in making a healthy mind and a healthy body. Healthy body is due to healthy mind and vice versa. In healthy body, positive emotions are generated by healthy mind. Reciprocally, endocrine glands produce such secretions as a result of which

S. R. Bhatt, *Jainism for a New World Order*,
https://doi.org/10.1007/978-981-33-4041-1_5

human being gets robust physical health and sound mental health. Vegetarianism has tremendously significant role in giving rise to healthy mind free from rashness and impulsiveness and in generating healthy emotions and healthy body.

Vegetarianism means non-violent food which does not involve killing or destruction of life, and non-vegetarianism means violence-generated food. In the spiritual culture of India eating of meat, eggs, fishes, etc., is discouraged and vegetarianism is enjoined. Āyurveda (Science of healthy and prolonged life) and Naturopathy have always regarded vegetarianism as health accelerating food. Now modern science of hygiene and medicine is also supporting vegetarianism. On the basis of several researches, it has been concluded that vegetarian is the best food which provides physical, mental and emotional health. By this, the mentality of violence and crime is subdued or curbed. In this way for the well-being of the entire humanity, every forward step towards vegetarianism moves us towards universal fellowship, world peace and environmental protection.

Importance of Human Body

The first and foundational constituent element of life is body. The vibrations of life are exhibited through body only. The flower of life becomes fragrant only through the symphony of respiratory senses (*svāsa indriyas)*, vital energy *(prāṇa),* mind (*mana*), intellect or psyche (*citta*), emotion (*bhāva*), consciousness (*cetanā*) and action (*karma*) in human body. In this worldly life, the basis of action is body. The experience of physical pleasure and pain takes place only through its medium. For the path of indulgence in worldly life (*pravṛtti*), and for withdrawal from worldly life (*nivṛtti*), the way is prepared by body only.

Types of Body

There are three types of body as below:

1. Gross physical body is that which is made up of five material elements which are fundamental constituents of body.
2. Luminous body is subtle body.
3. *Karmic* body is subtlest body which is made of *karmic* particles.

Luminous and *karmic* bodies always accompany soul in its worldly impure state and continue to be associated with it so long as the soul does not become completely purified. At the time of death only, the gross body gets destroyed. The subtle and the subtler bodies do not get destroyed. All these three bodies have intimate relationship with health. Even though till now subtle and subtler bodies have not been seen even by powerful microscopic instruments, and only some mysteries of the gross body have been revealed, still the impact of these two bodies on the gross body can be experienced clearly.

The gross physical body which is the basic motivator of our life processes contains several characteristics within it. Its every constituent organ, even its smallest part, is unique. The significance of most important small parts is not generally attended by us.

In order to augment the capability of human body, there is contribution not only of conscious particles (*cetana paramāṇu*) but also of material elements. Whatever elements are there in the earth or in other planets, they are present in this body in solid, gaseous and watery forms.

Vital Energies and Diet

The gross physical body is the basic source of vital energies or life force. These vital energies work in harmony and mutual cooperation. The nourishment of vital energies depends on food. From food, energy is derived. Energy is powerhouse of our body which gets augmented by vital breaths. The Nature has given immense life force to every creature and plant to fight with diseases and germs of diseases. This life-giving natural life force is called natural immune system. This power of keeping body healthy and free from disease is the life force. By this power, heart beats and mind works with more subtle sensitivity than computer. Lungs remain continuously in working condition. Blood circulates in every vein. The movement of breaths, the throbbing of veins, the communication system of nerves, the functioning of liver, intestine, spleen, kidney secretion glands, etc., depends upon this life force. The proper management, regulation and control of all these depend upon this life force. When this force ceases, the light of life gets extinguished. From the point of view of health for the life force along with the vital energy, the mind is also very important. By mind alone, the emotions can get purified. Therefore, it can be said that if mind is healthy, then body is also healthy. The basis of purity of mind is vegetarianism.

Necessity of Food

Food is the first step in the relation of self with body. In other words, food is the beginning of life. There are two elements that are foundational to life—breathing and food. The chariot of life voyage moves on these two wheels. If the wheel of breath stops, the life voyage will also stop. If the wheel of food gets punctured, it takes a few days for the life voyage to come to an end. Not only human being every living creature in the world survives on breath and food. Even the tiniest member of the vegetation world also breathes, takes food and thereby lives. Hence, it is clear that the primary underlying substance of life is food.

Some creatures receive food in the first moment of their life in the womb of mother. This food is the powerful means of life force and is the foundational energy of our being. So long as this remains secured in stock, the living being continues to survive. It is this energy on the basis of which a person dumped under debris is found alive even after some days. In the state of exhaustion of this energy, a person may die.

Healthy Diet

According to Ayurveda, there are three guiding principles related to healthy diet, viz. *hita* (salutary), *mita* (balanced and limited) and *ṛta* (righteous as per the season). Each of them has its own significance.

Hitāhāra (Salutary food)

1. It should be strength-providing.
2. It should be capable of development of body, and increasing of memory and lifespan.
3. It should provide adequate warmth to the body.
4. It should be quickly digestible.
5. It should not be exciting.

Mitāhāra—It is light food in a controlled, balanced and fixed quantity by eating which even after one hour, it is not burdensome to the stomach, and by taking water stomach does not become heavy.

Ṛtāhāra—Taking righteous food in accordance with the season and climate. This is to maintain balance between internal ecology and external ecology.

In order to remain healthy and prevent diseases, it is necessary to follow these.

Fasting as Conducive to Health

For transformation of life-sustaining powers along with for purification of food, fasting is also good. The benefits of fasting are both spiritual and scientific. On this very basis, it has been put among the four types of austerity in food intake in the spiritual practice. The four types are—fasting, curtailing the amount of food, to cultivate control over palate and giving up fried and fatty food.

Thus, it is clear that for good health, it is essential both to have balanced diet and fasting. For the removal of physical disorders caused by diseases in the body, for acquiring good health and for realizing the mundane as well as spiritual powers in all religions, the importance of fasting has been accepted. Fasting is the infallible weapon for tolerance and for developing the power of determination and will power. It is the elimination of excrement and dirt gathered in the body. It is a natural result of removal of extraneous elements present in the body. Body gets rejuvenated after purification.

The practice of fasting affects the brain. This helps in upkeep of memory, perseverance and power of decision-making and mental balance. It increases red cells in place of white cells in the blood. Even old age is prevented. There is less pressure on cells, and this accelerates work efficiency. Foreign elements do not gather in the body. There is favourable effect on all organs. Kidneys function very actively during fasting. In many incurable diseases, miraculous effect of fasting has been observed. These are all scientific facts about fasting.

Avoidance of Food Late in Night

There is spiritual and hygienic significance of taking food before sunset. By eating while it is daytime, the heat of sun helps digestion of food. For a sound sleep, it is necessary that the stomach should be light. Food gets digested before sleep and this contributes to health.

Diseases due to Food

Food stuff alone causes most of diseases and therefore so long as full attention is not paid to diet till then all remedies, all health systems will continue to fail. Many beliefs about diet are wrong mainly because in them attention is paid only to taste or nutritious qualities of food stuff but no attention is paid as to how much they are capable of complete excretion, cleanliness of bowels and health producing power. Eating of right type of food is important but much more important is excretion at proper time. Generally, the non-essential part of food is excreted after twenty-four hours. And at the most, it must get out in three days time. But if it remains in the intestine even after this period, then it develops bulk, laziness, dullness and intellectual weakness.

Large intestine extricates excreta. In its slackness, there are four chief reasons:

1. Ageing: Advancing age affects all bodily parts and thus causes sluggishness in the intestines as well. The vibration of intestinal capacity gets reinforced by *yogamudrā* (a particular Yogic posture).
2. Cessation of the urge to evacuate: By not excreting at proper time, the intestine stops giving signals to extricate.
3. Excessive food: By taking excessive food, intestines become sluggish. They cannot move or push off the excreta forward.

4. Eating non-vegetarian food: In the absence of needed fibre for digestion, the excreta gets glued to intestines and this also hinders the process of excretion.

Because of these reasons, diseases like constipation, uneasiness, fatness (obesity), gastric trouble, etc., originate. Therefore, food discrimination is very essential from spiritual, medical and scientific points of view so that as a result of this the processes of taking food and of excreting continue smoothly and poisonous elements (toxins) do not gather or get deposited in the body in excess. Then, there is no danger of any fatal or severe disease, and we can remain healthy and live a long and contended life.

Science of Nutrition

We take food and water every day to get the energy needed for fulfilment of bodily requirements, for conducting the bodily movements and for physical growth. For the sake of taste or for eating to survive under the force of circumstances, a human being may consume various types of eatables but for proper growth, development and health, and it is very much essential to have balancing of nutritional elements. Balanced diet consists of protein, carbohydrate and fats along with vitamins, minerals, salts and sufficient quantity of water. In addition to these, some fibrous material is also required for rhythmic alternating contraction and relaxation of smooth digestive muscles that forces food ahead through the intestinal tract in the form of peristaltic waves. Study of the science of nutrition helps us in selecting balanced diet, and as per its instructions we may take vegetarian balanced food and definitely lead a healthy life.

Basic Elements of Food

We get all basic stuff for our eating and drinking from earth only. The mother earth blesses the entire living world by producing grains and all other eating material. It is a truth ascertained by scientific analysis that in eatable stuff the basic elements of earth are present. All basic elements which are available in earth or in a lump of clay are also available in food stuff which is the base of our life. When due to ignorance or carelessness we do not fulfil the bodily requirements, then the deficiency of these elements expresses its reaction in the body and that state is known as sickness and the state of balance of these elements is called health. Thus, food is most essential necessity of life. In order to keep body healthy, every human has to take food but it is one thing to take food and quite another to take food with ratiocinative discrimination.

Why Non-vegetarianism Should Be Rejected?

Since human being is non-violent or inoffensive by nature, therefore non-violent food alone is his/her instinctive inclination. The initial period of his/her birth is spent only with mother's milk, milk of cow or buffalo or she-goat, grains, fruits and vegetables. This is normal food of the baby, whereas taking non-vegetarian diet is taught with specific intension.

The question is even though human being is vegetarian by natural tendencies and physical constitution yet why does human being of vegetarian instinct take non-vegetarian food. The primitive human being who was eating roots, leaves and fruits of plants and trees learnt hunting and eating meat in the want of easy availability of vegetarian stuff. But now situation has changed. Non-vegetarian food is unnatural. In extreme cold temperature, there is non-availability of vegetarian food and therefore North Pole inhabitants are required to take meat for survival but thereby their body becomes deshaped and mind dull. Today, when there is plenty of vegetarian stuff available and there is rapid transportation, it will be a sign of good future that these people turn to vegetarian food.

Non-vegetarian food reduces power of perseverance and produces unnatural excitement. It destroys the flexibility of arteries and bodily tissues and reduces longevity. As a natural consequence of non-vegetarian food cruelty, instant impulsiveness and impatience perturb human being. Therefore, for reformation of inner tendencies, it is absolutely necessary to negate non-vegetarianism. The human being aspiring for universal peace has first to give up non-vegetarianism. By that alone, inner tendencies will be transformed. Slowly many problems will get solved. For this peaceful and pure mind is necessary so that excitements are lessened. This is possible only by food discrimination. Merciless killing of sentient creatures is a cruel act. Therefore, from the points of view necessity, inner tendencies and compassion prohibition of non-vegetarianism is a very important element in food discrimination.

Vegetarianism as Disease Deterrent

Another worth mentioning point for rejection of non-vegetarianism is caution by scientists and doctors. Today from every corner of the world, scientists and doctors are giving this warning that non-vegetarianism is a cause of incurable diseases like cancer, etc. It decreases lifespan, whereas vegetarianism gives more nutrition and ability to fight diseases. High fibre diet which primarily consists of vegetables and food grains has protective influence from diseases. This happens so because there is no prior proper examination in the meat of animals about the germs of diseases developing in their body. Vegetables and fruits can easily be washed before human consumption but not meat. So, germs enter the body of one who eats meat of diseased animals. The tension, fear, restiveness, anger, etc., arising out of painful and cruel atmosphere in which they are butchered make the meat of animals poisonous. That poisonous diseased meat goes in the stomach of the meat eater and makes him/her victim of incurable diseases. From the modern studies regarding diet, it is known that from non-vegetarian diet human beings have more harm than benefits. Many doctors and scientists have declared that non-vegetarian food generates toxins in the body. Toxin obstructs blood circulation which invites heart diseases and other ailments. By taking non-vegetarian food, human being adopts animalistic tendencies, whether it is bomb explosion, terrorism, murder or gang rape. That is why Indian wisdom has negated non-vegetarianism for centuries together and will continue to do so. It is good that in modern times, vegetarianism is gradually taking the shape of a movement.

Advantages of Vegetarian Food

Our life begins with food. Because of food, other inclinations, tendencies and activities begin. As is the tendency so will be the mental impressions (*samskāra)*, as are the mental impressions so will be thoughts and as are thoughts so will be conduct. Conduct is the test of human being. On that basis, he/she is evaluated and his/her image is formed. That is why the upholders of dharma have given primacy to purity of food. It is evident that at the back of negation of non-vegetarian food, there is the consideration of lessening of violence, maintenance of health, producing of pure and *sāttvika* mental impressions and thoughts.

There is tremendous propaganda in favour of non-vegetarianism, but modern physiologists, nutritionists and health scientists regard non-vegetarian food as defective on the basis of researches. It is harmful from both physical and mental angles. From the point of view of human physical constitution also, it is evident that human can easily procure and digest only vegetarian stuff. Here one fact worth mentioning is that except human being no other creature in the world behaves contrary to physical constitution and mould given by Nature. A lion even if hungry does not take vegetarian food and a cow even if hungry does not take non-vegetarian food because that is not the food in accordance with their nature and temper. Non-vegetarian creatures spend their entire life taking non-vegetarian food. For them, this is complete food. But no human being can survive without vegetarian food for more than two-three weeks because meat eating will generate so much of acids and toxins that the very function of body management will be damaged. Those humans who eat non-vegetarian food against their nature they also have to take some vegetarian food because for human being non-vegetarian food is incomplete and reduces longevity. A vegetarian does not eat non-vegetarian stuff but non-vegetarian does take grains, fruits, vegetables, etc. The minimum requirement of vegetarian stuff cannot be avoided. There is no other stuff where completely balance diet is available as an alternative to vegetarian food.

Another point is that no one gets nausea out of disgust by looking at fruits, grains, vegetables, etc., whereas seeing hanging meat most people feel disgusted. Is this not an indication of his/her natural vegetarian instinct? Those people who are non-vegetarian do not themselves go to butchery. If they go there, then looking at the atmosphere there perhaps it will be difficult for them to eat meat.

Vegetarianism: Environment Protecting Food

Vegetarianism is such a diet that by spreading it there can easily be protection of earth and stoppage of desertification. On account of spoiled environment, the very existence of human being is in danger of extinction. The fact is that vegetarianism is a necessary condition for balanced natural environment because by this misuse of natural resources is stopped. Therefore, non-vegetarian food is completely anti-environment. If we have to save the tottering ecological balance and polluted environment, then we shall have to give up meat eating.

On vegetarian diet, a person can easily live full and long life. Vegetarian food provides health and longevity to an individual. It is a false notion that vegetarian food does not give stamina. With vegetarian food, we can get all the necessary nutritional elements for the body so that we can be healthy physically, mentally, emotionally and socially. It is a wise saying that, 'Take vegetarian food and see innumerable springs in life'.

Vegetarianism and Non-violence

Non-violence, which is preached by all religions, can be obtained only by vegetarianism. Without non-violence, the religiosity of any religion is mere travesty and deceit. Compared to those who eat meat and eggs, vegetarians possess more non-violent attitude and other higher values like pious mind, righteous conduct and spiritual illumination. Vegetarianism is natural and normal food. In the practice of vegetarianism, nature-given cooperative existence is fully established.

Vegetarianism Cheaper from Economic Point of View

Being given by plentiful Nature and being easily available, vegetarian food is comparatively cheaper. The cost of vegetarian food is much lower as compared to non-vegetarian food. This apart non-vegetarian is easily perishable and cannot be preserved for long. Therefore, it is not cost effective.

Health Is National Treasure

Health is an index of splendour, prosperity and development of any nation. A diseased society can never cultivate well-cultured, well-civilized and well-developed citizens. Health is a treasure of a nation, and therefore it is a pious duty of every citizen to preserve and promote it. Non-vegetarian food generates unnatural excitement, reduces tolerance and diminishes lifespan by destroying the flexibility of arteries and nerves and thus becomes unhealthy.

Why to Adopt Vegetarianism?

Food is a necessity of our life but there is no necessity of eating something which is avoidable. It is very much clear that in vegetarianism there is very little violence, it is healthy, and it gives rise to *sāttvika* psyche and thoughts. All the three points do not favour non-vegetarianism. Therefore, from these points of view, non-vegetarianism does not fall under the category of necessity.

Meat is not natural food and that is why no assiduous creature of the world is non-vegetarian. Horse, ox, camel, elephant, etc., no one is non-vegetarian. Non-vegetarianism gives rise to *tāmasika* tendency by which there are increasing violence, conflicts, domestic quarrels, bloodshed, robbery, etc., in the society.

We should ponder over the question of non-vegetarianism from the point of view of inner psyche. By non-vegetarian food, human becomes sexy, angry, intolerant, crazy, cruel, heartless and violent. There are many incidents reported in the mass media as to how cruelly non-vegetarians commit murders and mercilessly destroy the dead body. After drinks and taking non-vegetarian food, many friends quarrel among themselves and loot and kill any one of them. All these are harmful results of non-vegetarianism. Comparing grains and meat, we find that meat eating makes human cruel. That is why rejection of non-vegetarian food and the need for vegetarianism are to be emphasized. The discussion on rejection of non-vegetarianism was done earlier on the basis of non-violence, and now it is being done from the point of view of inner instincts. Everyone wants that the flood of crimes should be stopped in the society. Thus, from the points of view of necessity and non-cruelty, non-vegetarianism cannot be acceptable.

Without giving up things which pervert the instincts, human consciousness cannot be purified. It is not easy to change the habits of individual but it is not so difficult. Human will and endeavour play an important role in transforming human person. By them human being can climb up the stairs of progress. For progress three things are needed: will, determination and effort. First of all, it should arise in the heart of human being a desire to transform and this is will. The will to give up non-vegetarianism may have arisen but its strengthening is to be done by determination. The important axiom of transformation of life is determination. The entire secret of progress of humankind lies in determination. Finally, there has to be effort.

The first obstacle in fulfilment of determination is mindset of individual himself. What is needed is the awakening of consciousness for non-violence in the child. Consciousness is very powerful. Human consciousness creates circumstances. It can change circumstances. Therefore, faith in vegetarianism has to be cultivated in consciousness. We call this as *bhāvanā* (psyche). In our *bhāvanā,* we have to first choose and decide that we have to give up non-vegetarianism and accept vegetarianism. This is *bhāvanā-yoga.* Whatever *bhāvanā* a person possesses he or she becomes like that, gets transformed as that. Therefore, we should cultivate the *bhāvanā* of being non-violent.

Training in Non-violence

For the success of movement for cessation of non-vegetarianism, it is necessary to have purification and transformation of total mindset. Since today, the whole environment is that of violence, and the entire publicity system is presenting talks, incidents and stories of violence. Nowhere, non-violence is seen in it. Training in non-violence and non-violent lifestyle can definitely help in the spread of vegetarianism.

Conclusion

In this way, by comparative study of consequences of vegetarianism and non-vegetarianism, it is clear that by non-vegetarianism there is decrease in mental patience and stability. It increases impulsiveness and cruelty and mercilessness and develops lower selfish feelings. It instigates passions. Therefore, we find that non-vegetarianism is a cause of increasing violence, inhumanity, foul deeds, etc., in the world apart from other harmful effects. It is duty of all of us to stop it. If we do not do this, our coming generations will have to suffer terrible consequences.

By way of conclusion, it can be said that we should get rid of this delusion that from vegetarian food we do not get proper quantity of protein or energy giving diet. From the researches, it is evident that from vegetarian food not only high quality of protein is acquired but in soybean and ground nut there is more protein than in meat or egg. If common pulses and green vegetables are used, then not only the requirement of protein is fulfilled but balanced diet is obtained which can make vegetarian healthier, stronger and of greater long life. Meat has no taste of its own. In it whatever spices, fats and other substances are mixed, they alone have taste, whereas vegetarian stuff like fruits, vegetables, dry fruits, etc., have their own taste. And they can be eaten without spices with great taste. Some vegetarian people also get vegetarian dishes prepared in the shape of birds and animals and eat them like non-vegetarian ones as if they are non-vegetarian. To take such vegetarian food is not bad from the point of view of health, but it is not so from emotional point of view because our feelings also stimulate actions. By taking such vegetarian food, the feeling is that we are enjoying food by cutting other creatures. This feeling will take us far away from qualities like non-violence, compassion, love and sooner or later it will make if not us then surely our coming generations non-vegetarian. Being influenced by the significance of vegetarianism, millions of people of the world are adopting vegetarianism for better and healthier life. Even though vegetarianism is yet to be on the royal road, it is definitely a golden pathway to bright future.

Suggested Readings

1. Mahaprajna, A. (2009). *Training in non-violence.* Jaipur: Anuvrat Global Organization.
2. Mahapragya, A. (2013). *Invitation to health* (Prof. S. R. Bhatt, Trans.). New Delhi: Adarsh Sahitya Sangh.
3. Mahapragya, A. (2004). *Mahavira's scripture of health* (S. Jagmohan, Trans.). Churu: Adarsh Sahitya Sangh.
4. Paul, F. (2017). *Food, feasts and faith: An encyclopedia of food culture in world religions.* Calefornia: ABC-CLIO.
5. Jain, Y. (2017). *The Jaina way of life: A guide to compassionate, healthy and happy living.* USA: Federation of Jain Associations of North America.

Chapter 6
Ethics of Knowledge, Value Entropy and Terrorism

Abstract Reflections on theories of Reality, knowledge and conduct are seminal contributions of Jainism. All the three are interrelated and constitute an organic unity. Preceded by right mindset and right knowledge, right conduct is known as *samyak cāritra* which stands for virtuous conduct. It is the pathway to self-purification and spiritual realization. For this Jainism prescribes two modes of ethical discipline. They are technically known as *samvara* and *nirjarā.* According to Jainism, it is *karma* which affects human character. Good *karma* results in pious life. For this, rigorous discipline is needed. Bad *karma* gives rise to vices, and it has to be avoided by right mode of living. At present, human individual, human society and world at large are suffering from the malaise of multiple vices, and this situation needs to be rectified. Jainism can offer a redeeming way out, a blue print of which is being provided in this chapter.

Keywords Value entropy · Violence · Terrorism · Knowledge · Proper education · *Samvara* · *Nirjarā*

Introduction

The present-day world is passing through a period which is beset with value crisis. This crisis has pervaded all the spheres of value realization. It is mirrored in the human beings right from childhood to old age in the form of aimlessness, indiscipline, unrest, strikes, violence, disobedience of authority, etc. What is needed is to make a deeper analysis of the problem so as to find out its very roots and to attempt to visualize whether a reform in human psyche through proper education, which is the most important and foundational sphere of value realization, can bring about its dissolution. Terrorism and murders, thefts and dacoity, deceits and rapes are the most glaring instances of spread of vices which has bedevilled human society. We have already discussed violence towards Nature in the earlier chapter. It has assumed dreadful magnitude. Here we shall concentrate on violence and other vices among the human beings and Jain approach to eliminate them.

S. R. Bhatt, *Jainism for a New World Order*,
https://doi.org/10.1007/978-981-33-4041-1_6

Value Entropy in Human Nature

We are painfully aware of the fact that there is all-round spread of vices in human society due to loss of virtues in human nature. A deeper penetration into the problem would reveal the fact that the present-day tendency of value negativism is a resultant phenomenon of the loss of faith in a moral and spiritual order. The inevitable consequence of such circumstances has been the disappearance of moral virtues and the spread of vices. As a matter of fact, these two phenomena are the two aspects of the same situation. In order to resolve the value crisis, two ways, to be employed simultaneously, have been suggested by the Jain thinkers. The first is that of prevention (*samvara*), i.e. to diagnose and eradicate the possible causes of the origin of vices. Technically, it is known as stoppage of inflow of *karmas*. The second is that of cure (*nirjarā*), that is to say, to provide morality a solid spiritual footing. It is known as destroying the accumulated *karmas*. Jainism is particularly concerned with virtuous life and eradication of vices. The Jain thinkers have delineated on this problem and have suggested concrete measures which need to be attended to.

Samyak Cāritra as Basis of Jain Ethics

Though human suffering has been perennial, the magnitude of present-day strife and stresses in the world has become alarmingly dangerous and calls for an urgent course of action. Jainism as a practical philosophy and viable mode of living offers a significant way out in putting forth the theory of *samyak cāritra* which we have discussed earlier. The basic tenets and beneficial practices of Jainism based on this theory deserve serious attention of all ratiocinative minds. Jainism has the potentiality to make noteworthy contributions in all spheres of life for the benefit of humanity in particular and for cosmic wellness in general, and therefore, it would be redeeming to pay due cognizance to its foundational ideas and practices.

Causes for Value Entropy

According to Jainism, vicious conduct is not natural to human being. It is mainly due to ignorance and consequent resultant past and present *karmas*. It gives rise to perverted nature. Soul of a living being is pure and becomes vicious due to adventitious factors. A psychological analysis of the pathological cases will bring home to us as to why vices are due to. There seem to be four main factors which occasion vices, viz. badness, madness, rashness and folly. We may briefly explain each one of these.

In some individuals, vices become inherent in their mental make-up due to influences of past *karmas*. They possess some such psychoontological qualities of '*tamas*' that they cannot do otherwise except evil. They may rejoice in doing evil, or, they may possess the ability to recognize evil as evil and yet may not desist from doing it. They may know the good and yet may lack the will to do it. Such people need both pathological treatment and remedial measures through proper education.

In some cases, human's evil deeds result from some sort of mental disease. Such people are not bad but only mad. They do not have the discriminative capacity and the power to foresee the consequences. Such people are to be treated medically and tactfully.

Some people, who are neither bad nor mad, tend to do evil, not voluntarily, but because they are compelled to do so by the force of circumstances. At the spur of the moment or even in calculative way, they commit crime. These people need proper counselling and conducive social circumstances. Their family and social conditions need to be improved.

But in most cases, evil is due to ignorance or folly. The Jain thinkers rightly opined that virtue is knowledge and vice is ignorance. The evil-doer does not know the evilness of his/her act; otherwise he/she would not have acted that way. So, it is the lack of knowledge, and not so much voluntary sinfulness that issues in bad conduct. Knowledge is the only panacea for such people.

The ratio of the first group is quite negligible, and these people can be checked by constant vigilance and can be deterred by strong counselling. It is difficult to reform them only through education or legislation. Those who fall under the second group should be sent to reformatories and treated psychologically. The people coming under the third category can be brought on the track by proper training and the improving their lot. The fourth group, which, as we have said, is the largest one, definitely requires a moral and spiritual training. All these groups provide the rationale for moral and spiritual instruction. For all these, proper education is also required.

Role of Knowledge and Education

Here, it may be argued that the sinner knows that it is bad to commit sin and yet he/she does it. So, it is not ignorance but wilfulness which is the cause of evil. But in such a view, the connotation of knowledge is misconceived. By knowledge, we do not mean mere intellectual awareness. It stands for wisdom which consists in practical sense of values. It is well said that by reading books, one does not become wise. So, a true knowledge must tell upon one's behaviour. There is no gap between genuine knowing and doing. There should be a conjunction of true knowledge and goodwill. One who knows the good cannot stop exercising it. If someone says that he/she knows the truth but does not have will to practise it, his/her knowledge is only superficial and not genuine. To know the good and not to act up to it is a psychological impossibility. A true knowledge of the good must stir the whole being of human. It must be illuminating. This is what the Jain thinkers have declared when they said that *samyak jñāna* inevitably leads to *samyak cāritra.*

From the above, it is evident that wisdom or genuine knowledge is not devoid of action, that it consists in a practical sense of values and that virtue being knowledge can be inculcated and acquired. What is needed is to train the individual in a proper way to know the good and to act up to it. And here comes the role of education. This is what is called the educational theory of goodness.

The various instruments of knowledge like audio-visuals, books and discourses, sharpening of intellect, adequate methodology, etc., do play their role in the acquisition of knowledge, but more important is the knower who uses these instruments. The moral and spiritual character of the knower influences his/her capacity of acquiring the truth. The greater is the purification of being, the more certain is knowledge.

The upshot of the above consideration is that the prime need of the day is socio-economic reform and a reorientation of our nature of education. Along with being job-oriented, it should also be character-oriented. If our system of education fails to turn over a human into fully realized human, it has outlived its utility and is more than dead weight. The Jain seers were all the while conscious of this fact that a man devoid of wisdom can never be noble (‘*Dhiyā vihino nahi yāti dhanyatām*’). So, the task of education must be to inculcate in human being wisdom or a practical sense of values. The words s*amskāra, samskṛti, sattva samśuddhi, viśuddhātmā*, etc., used in the context of education and educated beings suggest the true character of education and educated beings. All this emphasizes that wisdom can be acquired by him/her alone who has moral and spiritual qualifications. At present in the field of education, we concentrate only on the information-giving. The moral and spiritual character of the knower influences his capacity of acquiring the truth. The fivefold gradation of knowledge in the Jain epistemology all evinces the truth that the greater the purification of being, the more certain is knowledge.

Menace of Terrorism

Among the multiplicity of vices, the malaise of terrorism is most widespread. There seem to be two main reasons for this, one is injustice and poverty and the other is religious misinformation. So far as poverty is concerned, it is the responsibility of the society and state to provide job-oriented education so that everyone gets suitable livelihood. Education is an important tool not only for survival but also for quality of life in the competitive world. By cultivating life skills for vocational performance, it is a preparation for life, a living with dignity and joy, with economic self-sufficiency and material comforts, with mental peace and contentment. Thus, education is a liberating force from poverty and deprivations, stagnation and decadence. Education for good economic planning is essential. We shall discuss details of Jain approach to economics in a subsequent chapter. Present-day models of economy have resulted in profiteering, deprivation and injustice. This is one of the reasons for rise of bloodshed and terrorism and even wars for getting control over the natural resources. What is needed is compassionate and sustainable economics which caters to the needs of all. This necessitates moral foundation of economics.

Jain Ethics as a Panacea for Religious Fundamentalism and Violence

The other form of terrorism is in the name of religion, and it has acquired global dimension and needs deeper analysis. In fact every religion worth the name has to be true, good and beautiful. It has to be beneficial universally. No religion can be bad or harmful. A true adherence to religion must ensue in respect of others' life and others' ways of living. There are alternative pathways to the goals of life, and if we are sincere in our intentions and earnest in our efforts we can realize them in different ways. This is the essence of Indian culture, and this is also the message of all religions of the world. Religious pluralism is the hard fact of our existence, and we have to accept it. This acceptance is possible only if there is mutual understanding based on proper study of scriptures of different religions. This alone will entail interreligious respect and harmony. If we are aware of the basic principles of our own religion as also of others' religions, there cannot be conflicts in the name of religions. There is no such thing as religious conflicts in the sense of conflicts among religions. The so-called religious conflicts are conflicts among the misguided votaries of religions. Religions are mutually tolerant but not their misguided votaries. Here again comes the role of education. It is not religious education that is needed but education about religions. It is unfortunate that majority of the people are not only ignorant about others' religions but they are also ignorant about their own religion. It is this ignorance that is at the root of all conflicts. It is therefore an imperative need to undertake study of 'comparative religion' at different levels of education highlighting the essential unity among all religions. According to the Jain doctrine of *naya*, every religion is true from a particular perspective and useful under specific circumstances. The same is the case with philosophical theories. The Jain scriptures have advocated equal respect for all. This is a unique feature of Jainism which should be emulated by all contemporary Jain thinkers and adherents of Jainism. Unfortunately, this is not the case, with a few exceptions.

Jain Ethics a Means to Self-realization

Jain ethics culminates in self-realization. According to Jainism, individual self is pure and undefiled in its original nature. But due to ignorance and under the malignant influence of passions accruing from the association with *karmic* matter, it becomes defiled. Four types of passion are fundamental; they are anger, pride, deceit and greed. The doctrine of *karm*a also is basic to Jain ethics.

Suggested Readings

1. Mahaprajna, A. (Ed.). (1994). *Ācāro Bhāṣyam.* Ladnun: Jain Vishva Bharati.
2. Tulsi, A. (2013). *Religion, Anuvrat and human wellness.* Delhi: Adarsha Sahitya Sangha.
3. Tulsi, A. (1996). *The vision of a new society.* Churu: Adarsha Sahitya Sangha.
4. Tulsi, A. (2007). *Bhikṣu Nyāya Karṇikā (Bṛhadvṛtti).* Ladnun: Jain Vishva Bharati.
5. Dayanada, B. (1968). *Jain ethics.* Delhi: Motilal Banarsidass.
6. Jaini, P. (1979). *The Jaina path of purification.* Delhi: Motilal Banarsidass.
7. Tatia, N. (1951). *Studies in Jaina philosophy.* Varanasi: P.V. Research Institute.
8. Sogani, K. C. (1967). *Ethical doctrines in Jainsim.* Sholarpur: Jaina Samskriti Samrakshaka Sangha.

Chapter 7
Science, Religion and Spirituality

Abstract The objective of this chapter is to delineate on interrelationship among science, religion and spirituality from the Jain perspective which should also be the general universal perspective. All the three human enterprises deal with different aspects of multiple Reality, and there should not be any incompatibility among them. It has been argued here that religion and spirituality have to be scientific, and science has to be impregnated by religiosity and spirituality. Science deals with empirical life, and religion and spirituality are concerned with higher dimensions of our consciousness. All are needed to fulfil holistic human needs and aspirations. It is with these presuppositions the present chapter delineates upon the nature, scope, results and interrelation of science and spirituality/religion. It appreciates the basic difference between them but also calls for their mutual understanding, harmony and mutual complementarities in the service of humanity and the cosmos.

Keywords *Anekāntavāda* · *Syādvād* · Complementarity · Science · Religion · Spirituality

Introduction

Among the multiple manifestations of human consciousness, the three cognate realms of science, religion and spirituality play a significant role in human life. There was a time in India when all the three were in intimate relationship and served human being with immense benefits. Though they have distinct areas of operation, there has been no antagonism among them. They sprang from existential needs and worked in harmony. Like the Vedic tradition in Jainism also, we witness the same coordination. The Jain concepts and theories are scientific and spirituality oriented. Many Jain saints and scholars have recently highlighted this aspect of Jainism. They have pointed out complementarity among them. Unfortunately, in actual practice, Jains are more concerned with religious dogmas, creeds and rituals and forget about the science and spirituality underlying them. But in view of the present alarming global scenario, the noble ideas propounded in the Jain scriptures in this regard can help humanity to overcome the present sufferings. The symbiosis of the three is the need of the times. Since this harmony prevailed in the past, it is not difficult to revive that situation.

S. R. Bhatt, *Jainism for a New World Order*,
https://doi.org/10.1007/978-981-33-4041-1_7

In human life science, religion and spirituality play a significant role. All the three are cognate in their impact on human society but they differ in their content and sphear of operation. At present, science deals with material aspect of Reality, spirituality pertains to transcendental Reality, and religion is concerned with modes of approaching the Reality through devotion and worship. Science has empirical methodology for its operation different from this religion and spirituality have their source in the trans-empirical but they have their application in the empirical world. However, there should be no cleavage between science on the one hand and religion and spirituality on the other as all the three pertain to the same human nature. Religion and spirituality can also be distinguished but they have subtle overlapping. This is because religion tends to be externalized through institutions, creeds and dogmas, whereas spirituality is purely internal. Ethical norms are common to both but they are central to spirituality. In case of religion when rites and rituals, creeds and dogmas dominate, morality takes a back seat. In fitness of the situation, science, religion and spirituality must get correlated and their symbiosis is helpful for the realization of peace, prosperity and universal wellness.

Science Explained

The objective of science is to know the material or physical reality, the forces and phenomena of Nature and the laws underlying them. It aims at transforming Nature through technology for human comforts. The findings and results of science are empirically testable; experimentally verifiable; practically observable directly or indirectly and mathematically calculable. Under given set of controlled conditions, they are reproducible.

Advantages of Science

Science, along with technology, has been of immense help to human beings. It has given invaluable information, though not complete, about the physical world. It has undertaken great strides and made phenomenal achievements. It has opened up unprecedented new frontiers of knowledge concerning the material world. There is tremendous progress in scientific knowledge, and still there is constant growth going on in this respect. Science has been beneficial to human being. There have been many boons of science. With the help of sophisticated technology and unimaginable progress of scientific knowledge, it has made life more comfortable.

Limitations of Science

Science has its own limitations. In this context, we have to appreciate two things. There is no finality in scientific knowledge, and there is always a scope for uncertainty. Godel's theorems and Heisenberg's principle of uncertainty/indeterminacy are a testimony to this. This apart from the second law of thermodynamics, which is the law of entropy, has tremendous implications for us to be careful so far as growth of scientific knowledge is concerned. Both Acharya Mahaprgya and Dr. A. P. J. Abdul Kalam have argued that there can be no finality in science. No scientific theory can claim complete truth. So, laws of physics will have to be constantly reviewed.

Secondly, science has inherent shortcomings in terms of scope and methods of exploration and its misuse by perverted human beings. It has limited scope confined to matter. Because of its methodological limitations, it cannot explore consciousness or spirit or trans-empirical reality. It cannot generate life. Only life begets life. It cannot explain our own self and has not fully explained matter either. It cannot explain meaning and purpose of life. It may try to do so but it fails. Moreover, it can explain how certain events, actions and reactions, processes and occurrences take place but cannot explain why and perhaps for whom? Further it has not so far solved the ultimate riddles of life and cosmos or provided lasting solutions to human problems and miseries for which it wants to provide comforts. An important part of Reality remains untouched and unexplained. So, it gives a partial picture of Reality. There is an immeasurable world of inner life which is unreachable by science and for which only religion and spirituality can help.

Science is purported to be used to manage and transform Nature. Instead some scientists ignorantly talk of exploiting and mastering Nature. Human being can only help Nature to help him/her. He/she has to learn lessons of ecology not from science but from Nature itself and also from his/her real self. This is the real deep ecology. All else is shallow ecology which we talk of these days.

Science and Technology not Value Neutral

Another point to be noted is that science and scientific knowledge are value neutral only in so far as they are not put to use. But the moment they are employed through technology, they become value-laden. Then they stand in need of proper management since they can be conducive as well as detrimental to our well-being. The high value entropy civilization, war-mongering nations and harmful consumerism, etc., are the evil consequences of value negativism imposed on science and scientific enterprises. For this we have not to blame science but to ourselves.

Science has plunged the world into total anarchy being divorced from ethical and spiritual values. It has given rise to gigantic problems with no satisfactory solutions. Scientific discoveries and technological inventions have no doubt helped in making material life easy and happy but they have also caused terrible catastrophes endangering life. Science cannot be value neutral in all its facets. It can be a boon or a bane depending upon the way it is put to use. The ill effects of science are due to its misuse by short-sighted and narrow-minded scientists under the perverting influence of the political bosses or commercial interests. Rightly speaking, a scientist cannot and should not neglect the ethical and spiritual aspect of scientific discoveries. There is social and moral responsibility of a scientist. As quoted earlier, Prof. D.S. Kothari very pertinently remarks,

> Ours may be called an age of science but it is certainly not a scientific age. It is not an age of reason or rationality, not yet. That can only come when science and ahimsā equally find a place in man's thoughts and actions.[1]

He quotes A.N. Whiteheadin support who opines:

> It is no exaggeration to say that the future of civilization depends on the degree to which we can balance the forces of science and religion[2]

He further quotes Cyril Hinshelwood, who in his Presidential address to Royal Society, London, 1962 says:

> To deny the reality of the inner world is a flat negation of all that is immediate in existence; to minimize its significance is to depreciate the very purpose of living, and to explain it away as a product of natural selection is a plain fallacy.[3]

Fortunately, now in the quantum era science has undergone a revolution and has come nearer to spirituality. Here Jain perspective is very much helpful. Niels Bohr's principle of complementarity is comparable to and can be reinforced by *Anekāntavāda* of Jainism. According to *Anekāntavāda*, the cosmos is a whole which consists of opposites. These opposites do not cancel each other; instead they add up to make the whole. Both matter and antimatter coexist. They are coopposites. Laplace propounded the theory of scientific determinism on the lines of Newton's laws but this was controverted by Heisenberg in the theory of Uncertainty. This is explained by the Jain thinkers with the help of the concept of '*avaktavyam*'. This helps in sidetracking all dogmatism.

Contemporary Jain thinkers and scholars are working on scientific foundation of Jainism and they have come out with many parallels for mutual reinforcements.

Role of Religion

Among the multiple and variegated manifestations of human consciousness, the place and role of religion have been vital and significant having an unmitigated influence on human modes of thinking and ways of living. The expected role of religion in realization of fulfilment in human life and for devotion to a cause that gives our fragile and fugitive existence meaning and value does not require any justification. Religiosity seems to be an intrinsic element in human nature that arises from the experience of imperfection and finitude in human life. The fleeting and evanescent character of our existence gives rise to a feeling that we are lacking something, missing something and wanting something. Religion seems to come to our help to provide the needed supplementation. It is felt that it can provide the required solace and succor.

Ideally speaking, religion should stand for a series of logically organized steps in the spiritual journey of a human being to experience and realize the 'Truth' of one's own being and of the total Reality. It should be a process of self-realization and self-fulfilment. This is explained in Jainism in the theory of *Guṇasthānas.* It should be a means of fullest efflorescence of our potentialities and capabilities in the service of humanity in particular and of the entire cosmos in general. Though in its formulation religion is anthropocentric, in its outcome it should be cosmo-centric. This is what is really meant and implied by the Sanskrit word DHARMA. Religion has to sustain the total cosmos.

Religion has come to stay in human life but we have to think seriously as to what form of religion should be adhered to. Herein lies human wisdom and cosmic well-being. Like all human enterprises, religion has been evolved to serve human needs. Religion is expected to bring about peace and beatitude in individual life and harmony and solidarity in social life. These are the values of religion, and ideally speaking pursuit of religion is precisely for these purposes only.

Misuse of Religion

It is an undeniable fact that religion has great force, and it can bring about social change and development in right direction and be a binding factor for social solidarity. But it is also an incontrovertible fact of history that in being dogmatized and vulgarized mostly by misleading theology, orthodox religious votaries have played havocs and great wars have been fought in the name of religion, and the humanity has bled and suffered and is still doing so on account of misuse of religion. The malaise of sectarian fundamentalism, fanaticism and dogmatism has brought about disasters in social life. Instead of fostering unity, harmony and understanding religions have played into the hands of vested interests in generating discord, conflicts and disorders, and even now terrorism is rampant under the same pretext. In the name of religion, again, there have been intercommunal strife and struggles. They are not interreligious, as no one religion can come in conflict with another religion. Likewise, there have been intersectarian and intrasectarian conflicts and fights. All these are given religious colouring. They masquerade as religious but they are not religious. Such a situation cannot be conducive to social progress. This, of course, is not to deny the positive role of religion. The point, therefore, is that we have to be vigilant and exercise judicious discrimination between that which is religious and that which is not so. Attempts to misuse religion should be exposed and checked. Since religion has great motivating force, its misuse can be extremely detrimental to social harmony and social progress. So there is need to be vigilant.

Contemporary Jain thinkers like Acharya Tulsi, Acharya Mahapragya, Acharya Hastimalji, Acharya Gyan Sagaraji, etc., repeatedly exhorted for maintaining purity of religion. In their discourses, they have emphasized that religion should be understood and practised in its real form. Acharya Tulsi calls it as 'Effulgent form of Religion'.[4] *'Religiousness is the holiness of the heart',* he opines.[5] According to him, religion is a matter of both faith and intellect.[6] It is not a set of dogmas and creeds or rites and rituals or ceremonies. It is virtuosity and inner transformation. It is inner purity. Spirituality is its core. Such an understanding of religion leads to religious harmony. Religion means end of separateness.[7] All religions are different pathways leading to the same goal. They can also be compared to different branches of the same tree. Equability based on *syādvāda* ensures religious pluralism.[8]

Science and Religion Have to Go Hand in Hand

There can never be real opposition or inherent antagonism between science and religion if properly understood. They have to be partners for health and happiness, peace and prosperity. This has been pointed out by Acharya Mahapragya and Dr. A. P. J. Abdul Kalam, a great nuclear scientist of India. They have emphasized that religious nature of human must be recognized and cultivated with scientific spirit. Serious scientific researchers today are deeply religious.

Spirituality Explained

Spirituality is different from and yet correlated with both religion and science. It is virtuous living with the spirit of essential oneness of all existences. Acharya Tulsi applauds spirituality which is very much needed. However, he clarifies that it is not just our need but our nature. He explains essentials of spirituality as follows:

> Experience of fundamental unity with all resulting in universal love, friendship and amity. These generate virtuosity and self- restraint, harmony and orderliness, simplicity and moderation, eradication of greed and minimum desires. These help in cultivating ennobling and enlightening world view. Spirituality is a state of peacefulness which is possible through meditation and inner transformation.[11]

Essential unity of the entire reality is the basic presupposition and guiding principle of spiritualistic approach, and therefore, realization of that commonality has been postulated as the summum bonum of all existence. The spiritualistic vision has enjoined to experience the self in all beings and all beings in the self. It has exhorted us to get engaged in the welfare of all beings, with malice towards none and with friendliness and compassion for all. Only a heightened spirituality of Jain seers along with other Indian seers could make them project the lofty ideal of the entire world as a family and the pious longing of '*May everyone be happy. May everyone be without hunger and disease. May every one experience the good and the noble and let no one meet with suffering'. (Sarve bhavantu sukhiṇah, sarve santu nirāmayāh. Sarve bhadrāṇi paśyantu, mā kaścid duḥkhabhāgbhavet).* This is the thrust of Indian culture. Could there be any better vision of universal peace and plenitude?

This expression of spiritual unity is not a mere lofty ideal of utopian dream or empty talk. There have been examples of great souls who have practised this way of life. If some persons could practise it why others cannot do so? Even if it is a view of life, it is at the same time undoubtedly a desirable way of life. It may be difficult to practise it but it is not impossible to do so. It is unfortunate that it has by and large remained a vision only but this in no way diminishes its viability or desirability. Hypocrisy, deceit and contradictions are inherent in human nature but they are not incurable. Through proper education, it is possible to bridge the gulf between the theory and its practice.

In order to properly understand and appreciate the spiritual approach to life and Reality, one has to adopt an organismic viewpoint drawn from *anekāntavāda* which can have several forms, which are all alternative formulations of the same vision *(dṛṣṭi).* Various traditions, thinkers and scholars have used different expressions to verbalize this unique perception. This is spiritual vision *(ādhyātmika dṛṣṭi)*. This is not available to the materialistic worldly beings like us who are conditioned by a divisive mentality of 'I' and 'thou'. It requires a specific frame of mind, a *samyak dṛṣṭi* (enlightened consciousness) that can be cultivated by a proper training of body, will and intellect. Acharya Mahapragya has developed the method of '*Prekṣādhyāna*' for this. Different spiritualistic traditions have prescribed different schemes of *sādhanā* (modes of spiritual practice) for this. All mean to say the same thing but diversity of language has created conflicts among them.

The spiritualistic view can best be explained in terms of threefold approaches to Reality, i.e. spiritual, mental and physical which have existential but no valuational hierarchy. They have distinct status and role to play but each succeeding one is enveloped and accommodated in the preceding one. Here there is no incompatibility or conflict. There is gradual widening of the latter in the former. The spiritual is the most comprehensive. In a spiritual framework, the material and the mental have an important place and function. In spirituality, there is no denial of matter and material prosperity. Matter is the base and very precondition of all existence. But matter is not the sole reality or the apex reality. Further, matter needs to be refined and transformed into that which is compatible with the spiritual. This is because matter is exclusive, divisive and competitive, whereas the spiritual is unifying, shareable and cooperative. Matter is confinement in space and time but spirit is expansion beyond space and time. Narrowing of the self is material and widening of the self is spiritual. To be spiritual is not to renounce the body; it is only to renounce the sense of 'I' and 'mine'. It is self-opening. This is what should be meant by culture and civilization. The point is that denial of matter is lopsided and harmful but equally lopsided and harmful is denial of spirit. But one wonders how far this would be acceptable to our vision blinded by the dazzling light of materiality and scientism. In this context, it may not be irrelevant to point out that the modern model of development has originated in the background of materialistic and competitive, rather mutually conflicting conception of human beings and the universe. In the mechanistic–reductionist paradigm, not only is the spiritual dimension of human and cosmic existence discarded, it has also been wrongly assumed that the goal of human endeavour should be to have mastery, victory, domination and control over Nature. In zeal to conquer and subjugate Nature, there have been abuse, exploitation and defilement of Nature. The arrogant human being thinks that Nature must be bent to the will, benefit and use of human kind. Nature is of great value to us. It is kind and benevolent. It is grand and gracious. It is rich and bountiful. It delights in serving us and does so dispassionately. But Nature is also very tender and delicate. It feels shy of exploitation and reacts. When it reacts, it does so to make us rectify the wrongs we do to it. What Nature wants us is judicious use of its resources for progress and prosperity and not its uncared exploitation and destruction. It will provide us nourishment and peace only if we live in peace with it. Worship of Nature is the keynote of spiritual way of life. We have discussed this point earlier also.

The materialistic consumerist outlook has resulted in loss of harmony between human beings and Nature, disturbance of balance between human needs and natural resources, lack of coordination between the material and the spiritual dimensions of development and finally in the overall deterioration in quality of life. It has given rise to disparity and deprivation, imbalance and inequalities. There is no denying of the fact that due to science and technology, there has been tremendous material progress but the fruits of all this progress have not only been inequitably distributed, but they have also been counterproductive.

In the context of material development, spiritual perspective is positive and helpful. It embraces the vital concerns of life (i.e. *kāma*) and the means to secure them (i.e. *artha*). It is *abhyudaya,* i.e. all-round development which sustains and which is sustainable, because it is regulated by dharma through which there is proper management of all assets available to us both in terms of human possessions and material resources. Acquisition of material resources *(artha)* and their enjoyment *(kāma)* always requires proper management through dharma. This is because, as we said earlier, matter is exclusive, non-divisible and non-shareable. So, it stands in need of regulation by dharma for its balanced share ability. Indian culture has always denunciated pursuit of *artha* and *kāma* without being regulated by dharma. The Indian response to *Cārvāka* ideology and its almost total rejection is glaring example of this fact. The present-day consumerism is an unabashed revival of the discarded *Cārvāka* ideology which has been doing immense damage to human psyche.

Spiritual experience is not realizable through discursive reason. It is supra-rational but this should not mean that it is anti-reason. How can any talk about unity of existence be anti-reason? Reason functions through analysis, whereas spiritual experience is integral but why should analysis and synthesis be regarded as antagonistic or working at cross purposes? Of course, discursive reason can have no role in spiritual experience but this does not mean that we have to decry or deny the role of reason altogether.

Notwithstanding what is stated above, it must be stated that spiritual experience is extra-empirical in origin though it is very much applicable to the empirical realm. It is available to enlightened and realized souls only. In this sense, it can be regarded as *ārṣa jñāna* or *prātibha jñāna*. In this sense, it is extra-empirical and not amenable to human senses and reason. Empirical knowledge is the description of facts, and this description can be true or false or doubtful. Its veracity is contingent upon empirical verification. Spiritual experience, on the other hand, is prescriptive. It is an enlightenment about and realization of values. It cannot be evaluated in terms of empirical categories of true, false or doubtful as it does not describe facts. It can only be evaluated in terms of its desirability or otherwise or in terms of ought to be practised.

Spiritual experience is a value not in the empirical sense. It is a value par excellence. All other values are comprehended under it but they do not exhaust it. One may acquire all other values but absence of spiritual value makes one feel imperfect. This is the philosophy of universal love rooted in the premise of essential non-difference of all existences. It alone provides the stable and solid foundation to all other values. It alone is the intrinsic value, the summum bonum, all other values are only instrumental. It alone is universalizable as it is an end value, an absolute value, which can be prescribed unconditionally without exception.

Science and Spirituality

Having clarified the meaning of spirituality in Jain context, the relation between science and spirituality may briefly be touched. This has been an issue which has always remained controversial. It has been viewed differently depending on whether one takes a holistic view or a discursive and compartmentalized view of human existence, human knowledge and human value pursuits. Under the sway of rationality, more often than not, it has been said that the realms of science and spirituality are not only different but also incompatible. One is the realm of reason and the other is of faith or intuition. One is empirical and the other is trans-empirical and beyond reason. Under the blinding spell of tremendous achievements of science and technology, some people claiming to be knowledgeable eulogize science and decry spirituality. On the other side, there has been a reaction to this attitude of scientism and some people have gone to the extreme of arguing against the evanescent worth and ultimate futility of all attainments of science and technology. The ill effects of science and technology further provided a strong excuse for science negativism.

A spiritual approach steers clear of these extreme and lopsided positions. The reductionist approach of either sort does justice neither to the integral and unitive consciousness nor to concrete uniqueness of matter, both of which are equally foundational, significant and mutually complimentary. In a holistic view, one need not conceive any rift or chasm between science and spirituality.

Science and spirituality are quite different, and one should not mix up the two. They differ in their subject matter, methodology and results. Nevertheless, they are interrelated and complimentary. There is no exclusive 'either-or' between the two. One cannot be complete without the other. Acharya Tulsi emphasized the need of their coordination[12]. In a holistic approach, the two are not unrelated. Prof. D.S.

Kothari also avers the same.[13] He refers to Samana Suttam, which maintains that the inner and the outer worlds are not reducible from one to the other, but they are also not independent of each other. Unfortunately, present techno-scientific culture has alienated itself from spirituality and under religious dogmatism spirituality got alienated from science.

Spirituality and Science—Partners for Peace, Plenitude and Perfection

Science and spirituality have to join hands for material prosperity (*abhyudaya*) and spiritual enhancement (*niḥśreyas*) of the humankind. Paroding the Gītā we can say, where we have Kṛṣṇa representing spirituality and Arjuna representing science and technology there is sure success in the attainment of prosperity and realization of peace.

Spirituality and science have been handy to humankind, have been taken help of by human beings for good cause and have coexisted, sometimes with mutual reinforcement and sometimes with mutual hostility resulting in antagonism and acrimony, animosity and conflicts. The interrelation between the two has been problematic and troublesome partly because of vested interests and partly because of ignorance of the nature of the two. Both are later developments in human life with a crude beginning and gradual sophistication. Both have served human being for betterment but had adverse effects also. When properly used, they have been conducive to good and more peaceful living but have also been detrimental when misused. Both have inherent limitations and drawbacks which need to be improved upon by mutual supplementation and independently. Given sincerity and earnestness, it is possible to do so. Then instead of being fighting parties, they can be partners in peace, plenitude and perfection.

Strictly speaking, the problematic relation between spirituality and science has arisen only in the western context. In ancient India, there was no such phenomenon as religion in the western sense, and neither dharma nor *adhyātma* is religion since they stand for the entire view and way of life and not just a set of creeds and dogmas and a mode of devotion to and worship of the divine. Of course, now in India we do have religions under western influences. But even now for us, the problem of relation between science and spirituality is not acute. So, in a sense we are debating a western problem, an imported and borrowed problem, superimposed on us. But since we have owned it up, we have to discuss it.

In ancient India, we practised what may be called *anekāntavāda* both of the Vedic and the Jain variety. (*Ekam sat viprāḥ bahudhā vadanti* and *Anantadharmātmakam sat.*) Science was not pursued in isolation from humanities, social sciences and spirituality. In fact, there was no separation of this sort. Both partial and holistic approaches were adopted simultaneously. Distinctions are alright and must be entertained for classified treatment, but they are not to be mistaken for separation. There is no exclusive 'either-or' about them, as stated earlier. All branches of knowledge and human pursuits have need, importance, value and utility for humankind. They are to be pursued both simultaneously and successively as per the demands of the situation. All of them are useful, are means for betterment and have served humanity. So, nothing is to be discarded, overrated or undervalued. A living being is a body–mind complex animated by consciousness. All the three are to be attended to, catered to simultaneously as well as in succession. Life and reality defy bloodless thought categories and logical quandaries about simultaneity and succession. There is no watertight compartmentalization among body, mind and consciousness. There is reciprocity and mutual openness. This is a hard fact given to us in experience. The outer and the inner are two inseparable facets of the same reality. Then why to close our eyes to this fact and be lopsided in our understanding?

Nothing can be a better account of the interrelation of science and spirituality taken in a broader context as symbiosis of *vyavahāra* and *paramārtha*, *preyas* and *śreyas, abhyudaya* and *niḥśreyasa*, and such cognate pairs. The Jain thinkers highlight their successive nature. Only one who has fulfilled the empirical and renounced the ephemeral really becomes a fit receptacle of the spiritual fullness. This account is in keeping with different stages of life. It insists that empirical prosperity and spiritual realization are not to be practised in their mutual isolation, in spite of the fact that they are different. Both must be taken help of, one for worldly prosperity and the other for spiritual well-being. It says that those who practise one in exclusion of the other are in darkness and they are in greater darkness who pursue spirituality alone neglecting the empirical. The material is the arena for spiritual realization, and therefore, it has tremendous value and significance. *Artha* and *kāma* are the *puruṣārthas,* and science and technology are good means of their fulfilment. For *mokṣa,* we have to resort to spirituality. In the Jain community, we have the example of Rajchandra who had symbiotic coordination of *paramārtha* and *vyavahāra.*

Science and religion are congenial means conducive to human and cosmic well-being. Their distinct and conjoint pursuits are helpful and needed. Exclusiveness and excessiveness are to be avoided, and 'Middle Path' is to be followed. There should be no overzealous excitement, no overzealous advances, and balance is to be maintained. Empirical and trans-empirical do differ, and yet they are intimately related. For example, brain research is not the same as understanding consciousness, and there should be no category mistake in treating the two. The physical and non-physical are not the same; the quantum and consciousness are not the same. So, they are not to be mixed up, but at the same time their close and intimate relation and mutuality are also not to be overlooked. What is needed is insightful discrimination and synthesis.

Late President of the Republic of India A. P. J. Abdul Kalam along with late Acharya Mahapragya were great champions of complementarity of science and spirituality. They opined that mere spirituality or mere science is dangerous. Prof. D.S. Kothari also highlighted this point. According to Acharya Mahapragya, the technique of *Prekṣā Dhyāna* is the synthesis of science and spirituality.

Isolation of saints and scientists has been harmful to both and also to society and the cosmos. Any conflict among them is due to ignorance, false views and obstinacy.

The issues to be debated are how to correlate them, where to draw boundaries and limits. This requires mutual understanding, mutual appreciation, mutual acceptance and a consequent will to cooperate. This is possible through a new psyche, a change of mind set and a paradigm shift in values. Its precondition is that there should be no preconceived notions, no biases and prejudices, no superiority or inferiority complexes. Then only an open-minded dialogue is possible. Harmony and cooperation are always beneficial. It is hoped that joint enterprise along with separate ventures may open up new vistas, new horizons, new pathways and new truths.

The cleavage between science and spirituality has not been helpful to both as also to humanity and the cosmos. There is dire need for mutual understanding and conciliation. In fact, greatest scientists like Einstein, Max Plank, Schrödinger and many others, and likewise many great spiritual leaders and thinkers have voiced this feeling. The Reality is holistic, indivisible and integral. Reality is to be known and lived in the best possible way. For this, both science and spirituality can cooperate and join hands to understand Reality in a better and more perfect way. Their marriage may be helpful and conducive for universal well-being.

There is a need to make religion and spirituality scientific and also to spiritualize science. Religious and spiritual tenets and practices that are insensitive to Nature and all living beings cannot find acceptance for a critical mind. Likewise, science and technology which are immune to cosmic well-being cannot appeal to sane mind. Both need to be purified. Both have not to conflict and collide but to supplement and reinforce. From time to time, wise people should remind humanity about this truth. It is a welcome sign that contemporary Jain thinkers and scientists are alive to this requirement.

References

1. Kothari, D. S. (1977). *Some thoughts on science and religion* (p. 9). Delhi: Shri Raj Krishen Jaina Charitable Trust.
2. Ibid, 20
3. Ibid, 3
4. Tulsi, A., & Bhatt, S. R. (Ed.). (2013). *Religion, Anuvrata and human wellness* (p. 1). Adarsha Sahitya Sangha, Delhi.
5. Ibid, p. 2.
6. Ibid, p. 5.
7. Ibid, p. 13.
8. Ibid, p. 12.
9. Ibid, p. 14.
10. Ibid, pp. 14–15.
11. Ibid, p.
12. Tulsi, A. (1996). *The vision of a new society* (p. 178). Delhi: Adarsh Sahitya Sangha.
13. Kothari, D. S. (1977). *Science and religion* (p. 1). New Delhi: Sri Raj Krishen Jain Cheritable Trust.

Suggested Readings

14. Mahaprajna, A., & Abdul Kalam, A. P. J. (2008). *The Family and the Nation*. Delhi: Harper Collins Publishers and The India Today Group.
15. Mahaprajna, A., & Abdul Kalam, A. P. J. (2008). *Vijñāna Adhyātma ki Aor*. Ladnun: Jain Vishva Bharati Institute.
16. Tulsi, A., & Bhatt, S. R. (Eds.). (2013). *Religion, Anuvrat and human wellness*. Delhi: Adarsha Sahitya Sangha.
17. Prajna, C., & Kanta Samanta, S. (2017). *Scientific perspectives of Jainism*. Ladnun: Jain Vishva Bharati Institute.
18. Prajna, C. (2005). *Scientific vision Lord Mahavira*. Ladnun: Jain Vishva Bharati.
19. Galera, M. (2002). *Science in Jainism*. Ladnun: Jain Vishva Bharati Institute.
20. Galera, M. (2009). *Jain studies and science*. Ladnun: Jain Vishva Bharati Institute.
21. Kacchara, N. L. (2014). *Scientific explorations of Jain doctrines*. Delhi: Motilal Banarasidass.
22. Kacchara, N. L. (2018). *Living systems in Jainism: A scientific study*. Indore: Kundakunda Jnana pitha.
23. Kothari, D. S. (1977). *Some thoughts on science and religion*. Delhi: Shri Raj Krishen Jain Charitable Trust.
24. Mahendrakumar, M., & Jhaveri, J. S. (1992). *Darśana aur Vijñāna*. Ladnun: Jain Vishva Bharati Institute.
25. Mahendrakumar, M., & Jhaveri, J. S. (1994). *Neuroscience and Karma*. Ladnun: Jain Vishva Bharati Institute.
26. Muni Mahendrakumar and J.S. Jhaveri, 'Microcomology, Atom in Jain Philosophy & Modedrn Science',Jain Vishva Bharati Institute, 1995.

Chapter 8
Jain Perspective on Harmony of Religions and Religious Tolerance

Abstract One of the most burning problems the world is facing these days is religious fundamentalism and the consequent intolerance, terrorism and violence. In the present circumstances, thoughtful deliberation on this problem from the viewpoint of *anekāntavāda* may be of great help to redeem the situation and to develop firm belief that coexistence and mutual appreciation are the only way out. Therefore, the present chapter is extension from the previous chapter on this theme of topical importance. It aims at focusing on the prevalence of religiosity in humankind and giving it a desired direction for cosmic wellness. Every religion puts forth the noble ideals of peace, love, compassion and friendship in a spirit of coexistence and cooperation. Religiosity seems to be ingrained in human nature, and because of varied human psyche multiple religions have come to exist. Plurality of religions cannot be eliminated, and there cannot be one universal religion. So, the only way out is their coexistence with cordiality and harmony. It has to be recognized that there can be multiple conceptions of God and modes of worship. We have to reckon with this fact. Jain theory of *anekāntavāda* is helpful in cultivating such mindset. We need to understand basic tenets of our own religion and also those of other religions. Then, we shall come to appreciate that there is fundamental unity in their tenets in spite of differences in practice. Jain thinkers have upheld this point.

Keywords *Anekāntavāda* · Religious pluralism · Religious fundamentalism · Intolerance · Terrorism

Introduction

The present-day world is facing the menace of religious fundamentalism resulting in violence, bloodshed and terrorism. Religion seems to be the natural desire of human being. In its personal form, it is desirable and conducive to individual uplift and spiritual enhancement. But its institutional form tends to get degenerated into bigotry and fundamentalism. It has come into existence to serve human needs and aspirations, but in its perverted form it becomes detrimental to that. Generally, it is not used for its avowed purpose. No religion preaches hatred and violence. Any act of violence and terrorism is against the spirit of religion and should be depreciated,

S. R. Bhatt, *Jainism for a New World Order*,
https://doi.org/10.1007/978-981-33-4041-1_8

condemned and shunned. In a civilized society, such a misuse of religion has to be checked. This malady can be annihilated only by proper study and understanding of the fundamentals of the religions of the world in a spirit of *Syādvāda.* Religion should be allowed to be in the service of humanity in diverse ways. It is an undeniable fact that religion has great force and value, and it can be harnessed for peace, prosperity and beatitude in individual life, and be a binding force for social solidarity, harmony and cohesion. It has to unite and not to divide people. It has to inculcate love and not hatred. It will be relevant to quote Acharya Tulsi in this context who asks the following questions:

1. *'Is he who exploits others religious? He worships, performs external religious rites and yet hates. Can this combination attract an intellectual to religion?'*
2. *'Is he, who exploits others, religious? He has the feeling of pity and yet indulges in exploitation. Can this combination attract a thoughtful person to religion?'*

And he replies that-

> A religious person loves all and so he can hate none. He considers all creatures like himself and so he cannot think in terms of exploitation. He who hates and exploits others cannot be religious [1].

Real Meaning of Religion

Religion has been defined in very many ways as per one's understanding and belief system. Acharya Tulsi has beautifully summed up its essence as follows:

> Religion has been described and defined in different ways but the substance of all is that it means a practice to stay steadily in one's own self. This definition of religion is as internal as logical. Even he who considers himself to be irreligious is not averse to this definition. The alleged restlessness with religion is for that religion which is not touched with the inner essence. Intellectual conflict cannot be avoided where conduct is subordinated to worship or external rites. This is what leads man away from religion [2].

There cannot be a better approach to religion than this.

Acharya Tulsi regards religion as natural desire of man and states, '*After every activity man wants rest. It is nothing but going inside. The activities of body, speech and mind take man to the outer world, but after some time the mind wants to return inside, the speech courts silence, and the body seeks relaxation. The relaxation of the body, the silence of speech and the retreat of the mind inside means concentration. This is the natural form of the soul and this alone is religion*' [3].

Need for Religion

Religion seeks redemption from suffering, receiving of solace and succour and realization of bliss and beatitude. Ideally speaking, religion should be a means of fullest efflorescence of our potentialities and capabilities in the service of humanity in particular and of the entire cosmos in general.

Apart from the need and utility of religion for fragile and fugitive human existence and individual advancement, it is also useful for infirm and shaky social solidarity and social progress. Religion is an intrinsic element in human nature like sociality. Just as human life cannot be conceived without society, human existence also cannot have deeper meaning and value without religion.

Social Dimension of Religion

Religion is primarily a personal matter, but when institutionalized it has social dimension also. So, in an advanced society it should not be misused to cloud social concerns. It has come into existence to serve humanity, and it should be used for that purpose only. It is hoped that knowledgeable scholars and public will deliberate on these points and come out with some concrete measures for the needful.

Inevitability of Religion

Whatever be the form of religion, it has come to stay in the life of human and is exercising, much to our dismay, a pervasive and dominant influence in our individual and social life not only in sacred and esoteric sphere but also in secular and exoteric life. It is unexpectedly affecting the political and the economic life. With the rise of science and technology, it was felt that they would serve that purpose but there has been disillusionment on that account. In spite of their phenomenal success, they could not substitute religion. There seems to be no alternative between having religion and having no religion. The issue therefore is not religion or no religion but what kind of religion? Is it a religion of love, amity and fraternity or of power, privileges, discord and hatred? A corollary of this is what should be the role and function of religion in individual and social life of human being. Religion has come to stay in human life, but we have to think seriously as to what form of religion should be adhered to. Herein lay human wisdom and cosmic well-being.

Desirable Impact of Religion

Religion has great force, and it can bring about peace and beatitude in individual life and be a binding factor for social harmony and social solidarity. Like all human enterprises, religion has been evolved to serve human needs. These are the values of religion, and ideally speaking pursuit of religion is precisely for these purposes only.

We live in the age of science and rationalism and cannot be called upon to accept incredible dogmas and exclusive revelations. Religious tenets and practices that are insensitive to human ills and social crimes cannot appeal to a critical mind. Obscurantism of any sort cannot be tolerable. The spirit of science must lead to refinement and purity of religiosity and safeguard it from the perverting influence. It must lead to enhancement of religion enabling it to respond creatively and constructively to every challenge that humankind faces which science is unable to meet. Science and religion have not to collide and conflict but to supplement and reinforce. Acharya Mahapragya in his discourses highlighted this point and pursued it vigorously in his life. It is the binding responsibility of religious leaders as well as of the votaries to respond creatively and selflessly in thwarting evil elements and protecting and projecting the good. Then only, religion can restore its lost credibility and bring about confidence regarding its utility. Of course, to a credulous mind religion stands for an external institutionalized set of rituals and bunch of beliefs deeply inculcated by mythological stories and clever preachers. But such misconceived religious phenomena cannot be conducive to individual well-being and need to be rectified. Acharya Tulsi describes religiosity as 'holiness of the heart and pleads for effulgent form of religion [4].

Equability of All Religions

Equability of all religions is the message of *Syādvāda*. Every religion is an alternative approach to the same truth. This calls for acceptance of equability of all religions. This means we have to equalize our feelings. Acharya Tulsi very perceptively remarks, '*He alone whose attitude is non-absolutistic can take the true elements from all religions and reject the false ones in a perfectly detached manner*' [5]. According to him, corollary of *Syādvāda* is coexistence and its precondition is non-violence. He issues a word of caution. He writes, '*He who is conversant only with Syādvāda cannot have the equable feeling for all religions, but who has devotedly practiced non-violence can certainly do it*' [6]. But he laments, '*It is painful to observe that some Jain scholars have not been able to carry Syādvāda through. They entered the arena of discussion as the absolutistic philosophers have done. They did not have equable vision expected of them in the background of Syādvāda. So the result in the form of co-existence was not fruitful as it should have been*' [7]. It is hoped that this attitude towards religion will be highlighted all over the world following the Jain perspective.

Religion and Sect

Acharya Tulsi makes a clear distinction between religion and sect. He opines that the purpose of religion is to unify whereas the sects divide people [8]. Religion means end of separateness. The message of religion is love, friendliness and equality. In sects, enmity, opposition and inequality are often developed. Sects are not useless or undesirable if they follow *Syādvāda* and give up narrowness or exclusiveness. He equates religiosity with spirituality. He gives ten-point prerequisite of a religious person [9]. They are:

1. He who is tolerant can be religious. Intolerance leads to division, not to unity.
2. He who is mild and gentle can be religious. He does not disregard or insult anyone. Pride leads to disunity, not to harmony.
3. He who is upright and straightforward can be religious. Deceitful dealings lead not to unity but to division.
4. He who does not covet wealth can be religious. Greed leads to friction, not to unification.
5. He who is truthful can be religious. Falsehood leads to division, not to unity.
6. He who curbs his passions can be religious. Want of restraints leads never to unity, but ever to division.
7. He who is devoted to penances can be religious. Evil tendencies result in disunity, not unity.
8. He who is renunciatory can be religious. Acquisition leads not to unity but to disharmony.
9. He who is not infected with possessiveness can be religious. He is not attached to body. Attachment leads to division, not to unity.
10. He who is celibate and a master of his senses can be religious. Ardent longing for sensual pleasures leads to division, not to unity.

Religious Pluralism

Though religiosity may be alike in all human beings, religions are not one. This is how the off-repeated saying 'Religions are many but Religion is one' may be understood. So, we have a plurality of religions. But this should not obliterate the basic spirit of religiosity. Truth is one but its apprehensions may be many. Likewise, we have a plurality of religions. The ostensive variations among religions arise because different individuals and individual groups attempt to understand the fundamental religious truths in their own ways and adhere to them in different forms and modes. Thus, religions may differ on both theoretical tenets and practical creeds. This apart the final ascent to realize the One Absolute may also be unique and personal to each individual human being. The point to be noted is that there is diversity in human understanding of the divine, and there are different forms of religion like polytheism, henotheism, monotheism, pantheism, panentheism, theism, deism and the like. In modern times, even humanism and Marxism have been branded by some as religion. The word religion has been used both in a strict sense and in a loose sense. This complexity makes it difficult to define religion or to point out its precise nature. A true adherence to religion must ensue in respect for others' life and others' ways of living. There are alternative pathways to the goals of life, and if we are sincere in our intentions and earnest in our efforts, we can realize them in our own way. This is the essence of Indian culture, and this is also the message of all religions of the world.

Religious Pluralism and Secularism in India

Religious pluralism and secularism in the sense of equal respect for all religions and their mutual tolerance are engrained in the predominantly spiritualistic Indian culture ever since the Vedic times. India is like a many splendored mosaic of different religions, cultures and beliefs. The fact that different religious communities are all her integral parts is both a strength and glory. It is for us to make this diversity a source of unity rather than a factor for divisiveness. India is well known for her age-old catholicity of outlook and broadness of vision. The seers and sages have always preached cultural symbiosis and integration of diversities either in declaring multidimensional nature of Reality or in emphasizing that the same truth can be expressed in diverse ways. Mutuality and complementarity of all existences and hence their organic coexistence have been the keynote of Indian thought. Indian religious and other literature are replete with such ideas, and this is too evident to state.

The exceedingly deep religious sentiments of Indians and their unflagging commitments to their respective faiths cannot be denied or wiped out. It is a hard fact and we have to recognize it. In situation of religious pluralism, secularism has been the ideal and in cases of communal conflicts secularism alone has been put forth as a mode of conflict resolution. The history of Indian culture is full of evidences testifying propagation and practice of secularism as a mode of peaceful coexistence. No doubt secularism is a word of western origin, but we are using it in our own sense and in our own context as equality and equanimity of state in its approach towards different religions. So, in Indian context it has a definite meaning and a fixed connotation which is different from its original western negative sense of separation of power between state and church. It stands on the contrary for religious equality and liberty with certain equidistance of state in its dealings with different religions. So, Indian secularism is not antithesis of religious devoutness. Secularism, thus, cannot and does not mean that people should forget their religious heritage which is so very rich and diverse.

Religion is not only deeply rooted in the Indian psyche. India is essentially multireligious. She has the unique privilege of being the home of majority of religions of the world. Religious pluralism is the keynote of Indian culture, and religious tolerance is the bedrock of Indian spirituality. It is based on the belief that all religions are equally good and efficacious pathways to perfection or God realization. It stands for a complex interpretative process in which there is an adherence to one's own religion, a transcendence of religion, and yet there is a unification of multiple religions. It is a bridge between religions in a multi-religious society to cross over the barriers of their diversity.

Religious tolerance which is the essence of Indian secularism has to be highlighted by pointing out essential unity among all the religions. This requires mutual understanding and mutual appreciation. It has to be emphasized that in the context of global unity and multinational mutually supporting coexistence, secularism in the sense of respect for all religions is the cornerstone of an egalitarian and forward-looking civilized society. So, there is a need to have inter-religious dialogues with an open and unbiased mind to promote mutual understanding. Religious pluralism is the fact of modern life, and it has to be given due cognizance in our social fabric.

Importance of Comparative Religious Studies

This mutual understanding is possible if we are aware of the basic principles of our religion as well as religions of others. As stated earlier, it is an unfortunate situation that many people are not only not knowledgeable about other's religions; they are also ignorant of one's own religion. It is this ignorance which causes all conflicts. It is therefore necessary to undertake study of all religions highlighting the essential unity among all religions. It will be out of place to discuss here the nature, role, scope, parameters and methodology of such a study. Only its need and importance are to be underlined. Religious pluralism is the hard fact of our existence, and we have to accept it. This acceptance is possible only if there is mutual understanding based on proper study of scriptures of different religions. This alone will entail inter-religious respect and harmony. If we are aware of the basic principles of our own religion as also of others' religions, there cannot be conflicts in the name of religions. Religious tolerance has to be highlighted by pointing out essential unity among all the religions.

It needs to be emphasized that secularism in its positive sense is the cornerstone of an egalitarian society. If secularism flourishes in India, it is not because it is a chosen political creed of a few articulate individuals, but because it is a living tissue in the body of Indian culture drawing nourishment from the best of our ideas and ideals, beliefs and practices. In a religiously pluralistic society like ours, secularism is the only mode of thinking and living best suited to us. It consists in treating all religions alike and in assigning them their due place with sufficient regulations to check their undue interference in social, political and economic life of the country. It also calls for a constant reinterpretation and renewal within religion so as to promote compatibility and complimentarity between religious conceptions and prescriptions.

The fountainheads of Indian culture and heritage have been varied from ancient times to today, and the fact that they are professed and practised today should not make one to doubt their universal significance and meaning and universal appeal. They are the heritage of the whole humanity for all times.

Ever since the early times, religion as part of dharma has played a decisive role in the history of India. It is a hard fact and we have to recognize it. The history of Indian culture is full of evidences testifying propagation and practice of secularism as a mode of peaceful coexistence and a host of such other averments up to modern times have echoed on the Indian horizon. The Jain approach constitutes the core of Indian culture and provides a solid foundation to Indian secularism. It can give direction to frame policies and programmes of Indian education which can be emulated world over.

References

1. Tulsi, A., & Bhatt, S. R. (Eds.). (2013). *Religion Anuvrata and human wellness* (p. 2). Adrash Sahitya Sangh: Delhi.
2. Ibid, p. 2.
3. Ibid p. 1.
4. Ibid, p 12.
5. Ibid p. 8.
6. Ibid, p. 10.
7. Ibid, p. 10.
8. Ibid, pp. 13–14.
9. Ibid, pp.14–15.

Suggested Readings

10. Mahaprajna, Acharya. (2005). *Anekānta, Ahimsā aur Śānti*. Delhi: Adarsha Sahitya Sangha.
11. Mahaprajna, Acharya. (1999). *Bheda Mein Chipā Abheda*. Ladnun: Jain Vishva Bharati Institute.
12. Mahaprajna, Acharya. (2002). *Ekkīsavī Śatābdīi aur Jain Dharma*. Ladnun: Jain Vishva Bharati.
13. Mahaprajna, Acharya. (1994). *Astitva aur Ahimsā*. Ladnun: Jain Vishva Bharati.
14. Mahaprajna, A. (2008). *Yugin Samasyā aur Ahimsā*. Delhi: Adarsha Sahitya Sangha.
15. Tulsi, A., & Bhatt, S. R. (Eds.). (2013). *Religion Anuvrata and human wellness*. Adrash Sahitya Sangh: Delhi.
16. Tulsi, Acharya. (1950). *Jain Siddhānta Dīpikā*. Sardarsahar: Adarsha Sahitya Sangha.
17. Jain, H. (2004). *Contributions of Jain religion to Indian culture*. Ahmedabad: Sharadaben Chimanbhai Educational Research Centre.
18. Jain, J. P. (1944). *Religion and culture of the Jains*. Delhi: Bharatiya Jnanpitha Publication.
19. Kothari, D. S. (1977). *Some thoughts on science and religion*. Delhi: Shri Raj Krishen Jaina Charitable Trust.
20. Muniśri, N., Nagin, J. S. (Tr.). (1998). *Jaina Darśana (Jaina philosophy and religion)*. New Delhi: Motilal Banarasidass
21. Singh, Ramjee. (1993). *Jain perspective in philosophy and religion*. Varanasi: Parshvanath Shodhpitha.
22. Rampuria, S. C., & Kumar, R. A. (Eds.). (1996). *Facets of Jain philosophy, religion and culture: Anekāntavāda and Syādvāda*. Ladnun: Jain Vishva Bharati Institute.
23. Vikas, Sangave. (1999). *Aspects of Jaina religion*. Delhi: Bharatiya Jnanapith.

Chapter 9
Jain Model of Cultural Encounters, Confluences and Coexistence

Abstract In this age of globalization when the world has shrunk with fast means of mobility and communication network, there has been interaction among different cultures. There is inevitable cultural pluralism. Multiple cultures have come to coexist. This necessitates mutual respect and appreciation. Each culture is true and valuable in itself. Exchanges of ideas among them may enrich all and make them free from dogmatism and bigotry. Encounters among different cultures should not be for subjugation or subordination but for mutual give and take. This alone can ensure peace and prosperity.

Keywords Cultural pluralism · Cultural encounters · Cultural coexistence

Introduction

Culture is a state of being, a way of thinking, a mode of living and a set of commonly shared values, belief patterns, practices and efforts. It is a complex whole comprising knowledge, beliefs, conduct, morals, law, customs, artistic, scientific and technological pursuits, humanities and social sciences. It is an individual as well as social affair. It is a total heritage borne by a society. Cultural life consists in pursuit and realization of values that enhance quality of life of human being. Culture is a living phenomenon coming from the past like a tradition. It is a crystallization of material and spiritual wealth created and preserved by a group of people and a society. There can be no genuine progress without cultural backing and cultural regeneration preceding and consolidating it.

Culture as All-Round Development

According to Jain thought, value realization and civilized living imply constant and all-round development. Culture in all its facets and dimensions is a crucial constituent and instrument of this development. It contributes to discovery of meaning of life and enhances quality of life. Thus, it enriches life, enlarges fullness of life, brings

S. R. Bhatt, *Jainism for a New World Order*,
https://doi.org/10.1007/978-981-33-4041-1_9

delight of mind and sharpens intellect and ushers in plenitude of peace. Therefore, culture has to work for these. But it is for human to live up to them or falter and fail.

Values and Culture

Culture is the basis of individual progress, social solidarity, national development and mutual cooperation. It stands for beliefs and practices and a value schema a country upholds and pursues. Quest for values and their gradual and graded and methodical realization have been prominent concerns and aspirations of humankind. This involves value schema based on concrete social and historical realities. It also calls for symbiosis of being, knowing and doing. Value schema is multilayered and multifaceted, involving the mundane and transmundane, empirical and trans-empirical, physical, vital, mental, intellectual and spiritual dimensions. It can be individual and social, and local, regional and global. All these are distinguishable but not separable. All these are to be pursued in simultaneity or in succession depending upon needs, requirements and situations. A value schema has four phases of end, means, modalities and realization. Knowledge of the end, proper acquisition of the means, skilful employment of the modalities and judicious utilization of the realized result are the prerequisites of a rational value pursuit. This means adequate management of reality situation, knowledge field, action programme and distribution system. In Indian culture, distinct and specific attention has been paid to their concerned theories of management keeping in view the unity and diversity of the nature of Reality and human existence.

Culture and Tradition

In all cultural traditions, emphasis is laid on utilization of past experiences as also experiences of others. The past is handed down to the present in the form of tradition. In this sense, tradition is rooted in culture. Tradition is a movement (*paramparā*). It is embedded in the past, it lives through the present, and it flows into the future. It is to be deeply rooted in the past, firmly footed in the present and judiciously embodying the glorious vision of the future. It is accumulative process of acquiring and transmitting, adjusting and applying lived experiences and embodied values and norms cherished in a culture. It is continuity as well as change. In a good and healthy tradition, there has to be judicious discrimination as to what is to be retained and what is to be discarded as dated and outlived. It thus admits of creative freedom and innovative changes. No culture can survive and thrive if its seminal ideas, key concepts and fundamental doctrines get fossilized and out-worn and do not admit of creative reinterpretation in keeping with the needs and aspiration of the time. Therefore, a constant reflective review of tradition is necessary; otherwise, it becomes a dead weight and burden on individual and society.

Diversity of Human Existence and Culture

As stated earlier, there is something unique and distinctive in each individual culture that gets shared or may remain unshared at trans-geographical spheres. In the process of sharing, there are encounters and confluences, submerging or overpowering or retention of identities. The values posited and pursued in each individual culture are global and universalizable, and yet the ways they are posited, pursued and realized are uniquely local to its culture. There is bewildering diversity, and yet there is striking similarity. The universe is also a multiverse. It is a cosmos with a natural tendency of slipping into chaos. There is orderliness, but there is also disorder. It is *vicitra* (wondrous). But given the will, human rational mind is capable of bringing about a synthesis incorporating the best in all. This synthesis is not bulldozing of differences but bringing about an organic unity among them.

Cultural Pluralism

The multihued tapestry of world culture glitters with numerous shining strands right from the dawn of human civilization. The multiple cultures of the world are quite varied and astonishing. They display some commonalities as well as differences, similarities as well as dissimilarities. Without proper understanding and appreciation of these and without thorough grasp of these, one should not undertake generalizations and comparisons; otherwise, they may not be genuine and helpful. In this enterprise, one should take judicious care to avoid false antithesis and monolithic comparisons. However, the variety of cultures has broad similarities which may enable us to have mutual understanding and call for a need for coexistence with mutual reinforcements. They provide richness to human heritage and are valuable in themselves. In the world history, there has been ceaseless flow of several thought currents with new tributaries joining them. There is multiplicity embedded in unity, and therefore human civilization is comparable to a garland of varied and variegated flowers each contributing to the symbiosis of the mixed fragrance. It is like a symphony of the play of multiple musical instruments in an orchestra each contributing its melodious tune to the totality. Of course, there have been some jarring notes but they should be treated as aberrations rather than normal happenings. So, the point is that multiculturalism has come to stay.

It is a welcome feature that humankind is in possession of multiplicity of cultures each having its distinctive characteristics. In the present era of globalization when we aspire for the whole world being one global family, it would not be wise to talk in terms of 'clash of civilizations', since all cultures are of equal value and utility and complementary in character. The need of the day is cultural dialogues, mutual give and take, harmony and concord. There is a dire need to have a common platform for cultural dialogue so as to be benefitted by rich experiences of diverse societies. In this context, Jain theories of *anekānta, syādvāda* and *naya* can be helpful and provide the guiding light.

Multiculturalism is a basic plank of holistic view of Reality and life. It is the view of manifoldness and multifariousness which provides a basis for peaceful coexistence, corporate living, cooperative enterprises, mutual caring and sharing, judicious utilization of natural and human resources, interconnectedness of all existences and their reciprocity. The philosophy of inclusive pluralism, concomitance, concordance and coordination ensures adaptive flexibility and reconciliation of opposites that is very much needed these days. It is particularly helpful in intercultural dialogues, religious harmony, conflict resolution, social cohesion and peaceful living.

Indian Scene of Cultural Pluralism

Though cultural encounters and confluences have been universal phenomena, we take up only the Indian scenario for the present. Indian civilization provides the best example of cultural encounters, confluences and coexistence. There is an uninterrupted spiritual material culture that is uniquely its own which India is sharing with the rest of the world for more than 5000 years known in human history. It is multifarious and manifold. It is living and has vitality to live. It is multiplicity springing from unity. In a comparative view of multiplicity-in-unity, there are two approaches possible, viz. to see the commonalities or to emphasize the differences. In a judicious view, both are valuable and helpful, if they are taken in a balanced way with a holistic and integral perspective. The healthy and positive approach is to see the underlying commonality which nourishes diversity as richness. But, if there is harping on differences ignoring the commonalities, there is occasion for clashes and conflicts. Then, it is not conducive to coexistence, mutual well-being, peace and harmony. Instead, if the emphasis is on affinities and meeting points, it leads to coexistence, mutual exchanges and cooperation. Thus, Indian culture is an integral whole in which different strands are interwoven with remarkable symmetry and symbiosis. But one should have the sense of apprehending them in a holistic perspective. It is for us to see the differences and discords or see the organic unity.

Since times immemorial, Indian culture has been characterized by the pursuit of two broad views of reality and ways of living, known as Vedic and *Śramaṇic*. Both have coexisted with criss-crossing and mutual give and take. Both tried to understand the nature of Reality for the betterment of human existence. The Vedic view exhorted to take recourse to supra-human trans-worldly forces also along with human endeavour, the forces which were believed to be operating in the universe. The supreme source of all powers was named as Brahman and such cognate terms. The human psychological infirmities gave impetus to this view. The *Śramaṇa* tradition, on the other hand, insisted on self-help, self-reliance and self-discipline. It rejected any resort to Creator God or supra-human agency. We have details of both these traditions in the Vedic, Jain, Buddhist and other ancient classical literature of India. In subsequent literature, also such references abound.

The *Śramaṇic* tradition has two main branches, viz. Jainism and Buddhism. Both the branches interacted between them and with the Vedic tradition. As discussed earlier, different schools of thought in India developed by way of mutual exchanges. No school of thought originated in cultural vacuum, and none developed in isolation or in closed compartments. It has been enjoined that truth can be approached, understood and expressed in diverse ways, and therefore the game of philosophizing can be played by mutual supplementations and complementarities. The development of philosophical thought in each school has not been in exclusion but in intimate interactions so much so that one cannot understand much less appreciate the classical schools of Indian thought without at the same time being well versed and steeped in the then prevailing systems. There can be mutual borrowings and corrections. There can be agreement to disagree. But there cannot be mutual ignoring or overlooking. Vedic, Jain and Buddhist thinkers are no exception to this rule of the game. There have been sharp and brilliant philosophical responses by and to them. Thinkers of each school undertook close encounters with the then prevalent ideas, theories and viewpoints and ably defended their position. Not only there are ample evidences of lively exchanges and resultant literature, but there are scores of treatises pertaining to *vāda vidhi*, art of debate and discussion, so that exchanges are meaningful and fruitful. They developed and perfected the mode of debate. The point to be noted is that all strands are complementary in character. They belong to the same genus and differ only as species. These differences are significant and of great worth since they provide variety and richness and therefore, they are to be valued. But they should not be exaggerated. There is mutual opposition, but this is not to be taken as hostility. The peculiarity of the Jain thinkers is that they have played the role of synchronizing different strands of thought.

Conclusion

Anekāntavāda is a unique contribution of Jainism which is noble and sublime, deep and subtle. It is not very easy to understand it and to practise it. But if this can be achieved, the world will be an ideal place to live in and to realize spiritual perfection. At the present juncture of time, there are value erosions, moral degeneration and different types of deprivations leading to tensions, strife and suffering. Besides, these problems arising out of globalization are also compelling the ratiocinative human mind to seek for new philosophy of life. With the emergence of global society in which we are interacting with people of different ideas and ideals, cultures and traditions, religious and moral norms, there arises the increasing need for a global ethics of mutuality and interdependence and intercultural dialogue for new set of appropriate interpersonal relationships. The ideas of global ethics and intercultural dialogues unfold themselves in the compassionate, rational and symbiotic Jain ethics of tolerance, interconnectivity and reciprocity and in the basic non-absolutistic postulates which preserve unity and diversity without undermining the identity of either of the two. The Jain tradition emphasizing *anekānta* (multidimensional approach to truth), syādvāda (contextual and situational approach to reality and knowledge) and *icchā-parimāṇa* (limitations of wants, possessions and consumption) is an important tributary of this mainstream idea which found sanctuary in the heritage of India and which is the main motif in the mosaic of Indian culture. Thus, Jain philosophy offers worthwhile perspectives on cultural coexistence and harmony.

Suggested Readings

1. Mahaprajna, Acharya. (2000). *Jain Darśana aur Anekānta*. Churu: Adarsha Sahitya Sanagha.
2. Tulsi, Acharya. (1996). *The vision of a new society*. Churu: Adarsha Sahitya Sangha.
3. Tulsi, Acharya. (2001). *Bhagwan Mahavira: life and philosophy*. Ladnun: Jain Vishva Bharati Institute.
4. Prajna, C., & Samanta, S. K. (2015). *Jainism in modern perspective*. Ladnun: Jaina Vishva Bharati Institute.
5. Jain, J. P. (1944). *Religion and culture of the Jains*. Delhi: Bharatiya Jnanapitha.
6. Jain, K. (1983). *The concept of Pañcaśīla in Indian thought*. Varanasi: P.V. Research Institute.
7. Sagarmal, J. (2002). *Peace, religious harmony and solution of world problems from Jain perspective*. Varanasi: Parshvanath Vidyapith.
8. Sagarmal, J., & Shriprakash, P. (1998). *Jainism in global perspective*. Varanasi: Parshvanath Vidyapith.
9. Jain, S., & Singh, A. K. (1994). *Aspects of Jainology* (Vol. I to IV). Parshvanath Vidyapith-Varanasi.
10. Jain, S. (1999). *Multi-dimensional application of Anekāntavāda*. Varanasi: Parshvanatha Vidhyapitha.
11. Aidan, R., & Shah, A. K. (2008). *Social cohesion: A Jain perspective*. London: Diverse Ethics Ltd.

Chapter 10
Role of Jainism in Evolving a New Paradigm of Global Economy

Abstract In this chapter, a blueprint is presented for global economy from Jain perspective. It is relative and compassionate model which can replace the present-day model which is not at all satisfactory. In the new paradigm, materialistic approach is tempered with spiritual orientation. It is based on spiritual globalization which is different from existing materialistic globalization. It is conducive to genuine sustainable development and judicious consumption. It is pro-Nature and environment-friendly. It ensures intragenerational and intergenerational justice. It is based on service motive rather than profit motive.

Keywords Ahimsā · Asteya · Aparigraha · Icchā-parimāṇa · Spiritual glaobalization

Introduction

It is universally realized that all is not well with the contemporary economic situation all over the world. There is no doubt tremendous material progress but the basic question is that has it been able to usher in the aspired peace and the desired prosperity at the physical, mental and spiritual levels? A large number of people are abject poverty-stricken. Some people do have enormous means of material and mental comforts but do they also not feel the evanescence of all this? The crux of the situation is that the present-day distracted humanity is suffering from and languishing in the narrow and rigid confinements of ego-centralism, parochialism, devastating competitiveness and disastrous materialistic consumerism. So long as one is entangled in the labyrinth of materialism, one does not feel the pinch of it. But the moment one gets out of it, one feels exhausted and lost. It is a paradoxical feeling of having and not-having, of likes and dislikes, of contentment and discontentment, of seeking and shunning.

S. R. Bhatt, *Jainism for a New World Order*,
https://doi.org/10.1007/978-981-33-4041-1_10

Need for Paradigm Shift

Apart from the above stated melancholy situation, we are beset with a global economic slowdown and this may result in collapse as well. In today's shrunk world, members of remote clans have now become immediate neighbours, in both actual and virtual realities. With the emergence of such a global society arises the increasing need for a global industrial and business ethics and multinational dialogue. Traditional financial systems were developed primarily to deal with human relationships within a particular social group. In this global society, however, we are more and more interacting with people of different nations with variant ideals, ideas, cultures and customs. There is a need to evolve a new paradigm of economics in the form of global economy of mutuality and interdependence, of reciprocity and exchange, of mutual care and share which can enable us to deal with such entirely new set of circumstances in an appropriate way. There are problems arising due to globalization which are also compelling the thinkers of today to seek for new model of economic planning, financial management and industrial production, distribution and consumption. 'Vocal for local' is a new slogan put forth to counteract the ill effects of materialistic globalization.

It is deeply felt that the present-day thoughts and practices in the sphere of economics are engulfing the entire world in a severe crisis, and therefore, this calls for sober thinking as to what ails the prevailing states of affair and how to rectify the root causes of the problems facing the humankind. In view of urgency of the situation, apparent symptoms are to be attended, root causes are to be discerned, and curative measures are to be adopted. But first, it is imperative to go to the root causes and undertake preventive and remedial measures. This necessitates rethinking about economic principles, policies, planning and programmes.

There should be no denial of the fact that the inquisitive mind is looking for a redeeming knowledge. The western economic thought seems to have reached a point of saturation resulting in a global economic turmoil. Therefore, it calls for a bold initiative for paradigm shift for which some directions can come from the classical Jain thought. The Jain approach is that of a moderate economy based on 'Middle Path' which is sustainable both in production and consumption that are the two aspects of economic planning and development. The Jain way is an economy of balanced development, balancing different pairs like production and consumption, individual and society, nation and universe, material and spiritual, present and future and so forth. It is holistic and integral approach to economic issues from micro and macroperspectives, which measures development in terms of prosperity, health and happiness of the present and the future generations. It provides for a cosmo-friendly economy in which instrumental and intrinsic goods are put in a symmetrical and balanced harmony. It is an economy of compassion and communion, of peace and non-violence.

Jain Model of Economy

Jainism in consonance with general Indian culture has the possibility of providing an alternative which may prove to be a remedial measure. Full details can be worked out on the basis of the seminal ideas presented here, as only a blueprint is provided at this juncture for perusal of concerned and interested scholars. In this respect, some basic guiding principles have already been very pertinently pointed out by Acharya Tulsi and Acharya Mahapragya. The ideas of global economics, multinational exchanges, equality and peaceful coexistence unfold themselves in the compassionate, rational and symbiotic Jain ethics of tolerance, interdependence and reciprocity and in the basic pluralistic postulates which preserve unity and diversity without undermining the distinct identity of the whole and the parts.

In the midst of discovering the global interdependence and mutual interrelationship, we are required to participate in the modern experience of global coexistence which marks a new phase in the human quest to discover our full humanity. To achieve this goal, Jainism has given the principles like *ahimsā, asteya, aparigrah, hita, śubha, lābha, yoga, kṣema* and *icchā-parimāṇa* to share with the world. Each of these principles has power to give new shape to present ways of thinking and living and bring people of different cultures, traditions, philosophies, ideologies and values under one umbrella without removing their particular identity. Today, in the time of crises of diverse type, Jainism can play an important role to evolve a new paradigm of economics, which can fulfil the contemporary needs and aspirations and can show a bright and beneficial path of progress to the world. The Jain approach to structure and manage economy at national and global levels can offer an effective and more beneficial alternative to the present-day individualistic, materialistic, consumerist, profit-seeking and competitive economy.

Jain economy is essentially characterized by love and compassion, benevolence and altruism, interdependence and interrelation, mutual openness and reciprocity, fellowship and participation, giving and renouncing, caring and sharing. Jainism does provide guiding principles on which economic thought and planning and economic behaviour of individual, society and state can be based. It is an integral and holistic approach which is organic and non-divisive. *Yoga* (supplementation of existing resources) and *kṣema* (protection of the present resources and preserving them from depletion) in production and *asteya* (consuming only that much which is absolutely needed ensuring intragenerational justice by fair distribution without depriving others) and *aparigraha* (not to overconsume and deprive the posterity for their legitimate needs and thus ensure intergenerational justice) in consumption are parts of skilful economic planning and behaviour. Jain economic thought is based on these principles, avoiding extremes of capitalism and communism, individualism and totalitarianism, poverty and affluence, self-negation and self-indulgence. It calls for consumption without consumerism. It accepts profit without profiteering. Profit is not to be used solely for personal purposes. Jain economy emphasizes social component with the ultimate goal of cosmic well-being. It repudiates competitive economy and calls for cooperative economy. It emphasizes the culture of 'giving' rather than the culture of 'having'. Thus, it offers a new rationality for a paradigm shift from exploitation to service, from hedonistic pleasure to spiritual enhancement. Jain approach to business ethics is not rights-based but obligation-oriented. It involves performance of one's obligations as per one's station in the total cosmic set-up. In order that one can perform one's duties properly, skilfully and efficiently one must know one's nature and capabilities as those of others and also what is to be performed, how to be performed, when to be performed, why to be performed, etc. But apart from this 'management of action', there is a need for the 'management of result of action'. It may be helpful to note that every purposive action has to be motivated but it has not to be intended. That is to say, the agent should know why the action is to be performed and what shall be its consequence. This apart he/she should have the will and skill to do so. But he should not be attached to the consequences or usurp them.

Compassionate Economy

Jain model of economy is that of caring and sharing. It is caring in the sense of judicious utilization of resources. It is equitable sharing of the production with minimal consumption. It is sharing with the present and with the future. This sharing means limitations of wants, desires and possessions, curb on unlimited cravings, unlimited accumulation and unlimited consumption and leaving natural resources for posterity. Acquisition of wealth is not bad, only attachment to it or its misuse is to be avoided. The guiding principle is, 'Use that which is needful and leave the surplus for future generation'. There has to be sustainable production and fair distribution. Everyone has equal right to share the natural resources and therefore there should be no deprivation.

Thus, Jain model stands for non-consumerist attitude wherein the policy is, there should be production only if needed and not first production and then arousal of needs as is the practice these days. The present-day policy of advertisement, allurement and seduction should be stopped. True renunciation is a state of mind of a human being. It is not only renunciation of unnecessary material goods or consumerist mindset but also evil thoughts and feelings, rigid attitudes and wrong beliefs.

Regenerative Economics

Apart from individual and social moral disciplines referred to above, we have to attend to world economic order which is closely related to and dependent upon the environment. The ignorance or failure of modern economic theory to acknowledge this fact has resulted in multiple ills and evils in the world. Because of exploitation and misuse of Nature, the growth attained under this model is unsustainable. This apart it has made human self-centred, greedy, insensitive and violent. Carelessness, selfishness, obstinacy and greed are the causes of this mindset. Their eradication requires cultivation of pious mind and practice of virtuous conduct. What is needed is a radical paradigm shift in economic planning and execution in the form of 'Regenerative Economics' and 'Compassionate Economics'.

Need for Cosmic Vision

The vision of self-sameness of all existences and zealous longing for eradication of sufferings of others as one's own cross all barriers of race, creed, country and even humanity. The benevolent teachings of universal compassion and cosmic goodwill, living and working for totality, all these have a significant message for the present-day distracted humankind. There is a dire need for a total transformation of our values, ideals, beliefs and attitudes. A time has come for the beginning of a cultural renaissance for which the holistic Jain teachings can play a vital and pivotal role.

This write-up has limited concerns and stems from the disillusionment with the dichotomous, exclusivist and lopsided economic situations that obtain in the modern world and outline a brief sketch of economic system as per the Jain approach to structure and manage economy at the national and global levels. It is hoped that the Jain thought can possibly offer an effective and more beneficial alternative to the present-day individualistic–materialistic–consumerist–profit-seeking–competitive–exploitative economy which is bereft of welfare contents, sustainability of economic resources and spiritual orientation. There is a need for reinterpretation of the seminal concepts referred to above in the context of production, distribution and consumption of material goods both for material prosperity (*preyas*) and spiritual enhancement (*śreyas*). This has to attend to all the four drivers of economic development, viz. human resources, natural resources, capital resources and innovative technology. Acharya Mahapragya has put forth some seminal ideas which need to be pondered over. The motivating factor in attempting this enterprise is that if we possess something which may prove helpful and useful to world peace, progress and plenitude, we should not hesitate in sharing it with the world at large. Rather than being burden to the world or being idle spectator to the universal suffering or feeling shy in sharing cultural heritage with others, we should attempt to partake in cooperative endeavour to resolve the problems of the world and creatively reconsider what our ancient culture and civilization can offer.

Suggested Readings

1. Mahapragya, A. (2008). *Economics of Mahaveer*. Delhi: Adarsha Sahitya Sangha.
2. Pragya, C. (2005). *Scientific vision of Mahavira*. Jain Vishva Bharti.
3. Jain, S., & Pandey, S. (1998). *Jainism in global perspective*. Parshvnath Vidyapith-Varanasi.
4. Reading, M. (2019). *The anuvrat movement: A case study of Jain-inspired ethical and eco-conscious living*. Switzerland: MDPI Journal.

5. Rankin, A., & Shah, A. (2018). *Jainism and ethical finance: A timeless business model*. London: Routledge.
6. Sogani, K. C. (2001). *Ethical doctrines in Jainism*. Solapur: Jain Sanskriti Samrakshak Sangh.

Chapter 11
Rethinking Democracy and a Plea for Dharmocracy

Abstract One of the most striking features of contemporary political scenario is widespread popularity of democracy so much so that many people think that there can be no other desirable alternative. They may argue that there is end of history/ideology and with democracy saturation point has reached in political thought. They may assume democracy to be the best form of government that can be conceived by human mind and think that no alternative to democracy is conceivable. There is an end to human rational capacity, and there can be no advancement beyond. 'Thus far and no further' position seems to be the point of culmination of thought to them. To a rational and creative human mind, it is irrational to think and talk of end of history or saturation in thinking. To ask reason not to think further is to ask it to commit suicide. Innovative thinking, transformative thinking and radical thinking should be regarded as natural to human mind. Therefore, with regard to political thinking also there must be rethinking about democracy leading to search for an alternative. To safeguard freedom and justice, we shall have to re-examine tenets of modern political thinking, premises upon which it is built and policies upon which it acts. The alternative may or may not be radically different, but it must surely be essentially different in the sense that it should transcend all the limitations, deformities, drawbacks and demerits of democracy, particularly the ones of the manifold forms of democracy practised in modern times. It is not a plea to distrust or reject but to re-examine it, to transform it, to cleanse it and if needed to go beyond it and look for an alternative. It is too well known to argue that all is not well with democracy. The search for an alternative requires newer intuitions, fresh insights and innovative thinking. If necessary, it may call for paradigm shift in end, means and modalities, and consequent structuring of new vocabulary and phraseology. Acharya Tulsi and Acharya Mahapragya have given thoughts to this issue and have provided helpful suggestions.

Keywords Democracy · *Dharmocracy* · Decentralization of power · Peoples' participation · Mahatma Gandhi · Acharya Tulsi · Acharya Mahapragya

S. R. Bhatt, *Jainism for a New World Order*,
https://doi.org/10.1007/978-981-33-4041-1_11

Introduction

These days, democracy as a form of political governance is prevalent in most of the countries of the world. It is believed that other forms of governance practised so far, or being practised, are either outdated or not good. History of political thought has witnessed several forms of political organizations ranging from autocracy to democracy. In the past monarchy, oligarchy, aristocracy, syndicalism and several other forms were prevalent as different modes of political organization and people were not satisfied with their functioning. Though monarchy still continues in some countries, it is mostly nominal and on the way out in favour of democracy which is the latest trend. Because it is most modern and has acquired some prestige and putative position, it is accepted without question.

Different Types of Democracy

Of democracy also we find various brands. There are most liberal as well as most dictatorial forms, and both call themselves democratic. Democracy is thus the most contested concept. Different people mean different things by democracy with the result that the word democracy has lost its meaning. In the name of democracy, the powers that be can do anything and everything for self-interest and self-aggrandizement. Opponents and dissenters can be crushed and wiped out. It is quite evident from history that the democratic England promoted colonialism and democratically elected heads of states or prime ministers have become dictators. We have people's democracy in which people are hardly involved in governance. We have liberal democracies that are most conservative and despotic. We have socialist democracies in which freedom, equality and justice are trampled with. We have deliberative democracy in which people hardly deliberate. We have guided democracy in which only one or a few persons guide the nation to assume powers. We have propagation of 'radical democracy', 'limited or lesser democracy' (Dr. Mahathir bin Mohamad of Malaysia), 'committed democracy' (Mrs. Indira Gandhi), 'controlled democracy', etc. But 'Purna Svaraj' of Mahatma Gandhi offers a genuine outline of 'Dharmic democracy' which can also be named as 'Dharmocracy' in which sovereignty of people is based on pure moral authority.

Defects of Democracy

It may be admitted that democracy is the best form of governance *evolved so far* but it cannot be said to be the best or that there can be or should be no scope for modification or improvement in its theoretical foundations and actual functioning. In view of the deficiencies and drawbacks in its functioning, it is necessary to revisit and examine the very foundations of democracy. It may involve drawing out new ideas and ideals and practices and disowning the prevalent ones that may not be useful or that may be obstructive.

Recently, Mahatma Gandhi, Pt. Deendayal Upadhyaya, Acharya Tulsi and Achraya Mahaprgya have voiced concern about malpractices prevalent under the umbrella of democracy. As Winston Churchill once remarked,

> No one pretends that democracy is perfect or all-wise. Indeed it has been said that democracy is the worst form of government except all those other forms that have been tried from time to time [1].

There is lot of truth in what Churchill opined. Plato's well-known objections to democracy that it puts power in the hands of ignorant and unwise people also cannot be overlooked. We cannot overlook critical views of Mahatma Gandhi in his seminal work 'Hind Swaraj' referring to British Parliamentary System of democracy. He opined that we consider British Parliamentary System to be '*the Mother of Parliaments but it is like a sterile woman and a prostitute. Both these are harsh terms, but exactly fit the case. That Parliament has not yet, of its own accord, done a single good thing. Hence I have compared it to a sterile woman. The natural condition of that Parliament is such that, without outside pressure, it can do nothing. It is like a prostitute because it is under the control of ministers who change from time to time. Today it is under Mr. Asquith, tomorrow it may be under Mr. Balfour*' [2].

Elaborating this he writes,

> The best men are supposed to be elected by the people. The members serve without pay and therefore, it must be assumed, only for the public weal. The electors are considered to be educated and therefore we should assume that they would not generally make mistakes in their choice. Such a Parliament should not need to spur of petitions or any other pressure. Its work should be so smooth that its effects would be more apparent day by day. But, as a matter of fact, it is generally acknowledged that the members are hypocritical and selfish. Each thinks of his own little interest. It is fear that is the guiding motive. What is done today may be undone tomorrow. It is not possible to recall a single instance in which finality can be predicted for its work. When the greatest questions are debated, its members have been seen to stretch themselves and to doze. Sometimes the members talk away until the listeners are disgusted. Carlyle has called it the "talking shop of the world". Members vote for their party without a thought. Their so-called discipline binds them to this it. If any member, by way of exception, gives an independent vote, he is considered a renegade. If the money and the time wasted by the Parliament were entrusted to a few good men, the English nation would be occupying today much higher position. Parliament is simply a costly toy of the nation. These views are by no means peculiar to me. Some great English thinkers have expressed them. One of the members of that Parliament recently said that a true Christian could not become a member of it. Another said that it was a baby. And if it has remained a baby even after an existence of seven hundred years, when will it outgrow its babyhood?

Explaining the epithet 'prostitute' he writes,

> Parliament is without a real master. Under the Prime Minister, its movement is not steady but it is buffeted about like a prostitute. The Prime Minister is more concerned about his power than about welfare of Parliament. His energy is concentrated upon securing the success of his party. His care is not always that Parliament should do right. Prime Ministers are known to have made Parliament do things merely for party advantage. All this is worth thinking

over.... In order to gain their ends, they certainly bribe people with honours. I do not hesitate to say that they have neither real honesty nor a living conscience [3].

About the English voters, Mahatma Gandhi wrote as follows:

To the English voters their newspaper is their bible. They take their cue from their newspapers which are often dishonest. The same fact is differently interpreted by different newspapers, according to the party in whose interests they are edited... [4].

He further writes,

These views swing like a pendulum of a clock and are never steadfast. The people would follow a powerful orator or a man who gives them parties, receptions etc. As are the people, so is their Parliament [5].

What Mahatma Gandhi held in 1908 that still holds good even now, and it may continue to be so unless there is radical review of functioning of democracy all over the globe.

Pandit Deendayal Upadhyaya in his lectures entitled ‘Integral Humanism’ very correctly opines about the functioning of democracy in India. He writes,

Consequently, opportunists with no principles reign in the politics of our country. Parties and politicians have neither principles nor aims nor a standard code of conduct. A person feels there is nothing wrong in leaving party and joining another. Even alliances and mergers of parties or their bifurcations are dictated not by agreements or differences in principles, but purely by gains in elections or in positions of power....Now there is complete license in politics. As a result, in public mind there is distrust for everyone. There is hardly any person whose integrity is beyond doubt in the public mind. This situation must be changed. Otherwise unity and discipline cannot be established in society [6].

Whatever is described above regarding England and India holds good about all other countries which practise democracy.

James Boward in his book ‘Freedom in Chains’ writes, ‘*The effort to find a political mechanism to force government to serve the people is modern search for the Holy Grail. Though no such mechanism has been found, government power has been relentlessly expanded anyhow*’ [7].

One may not fully agree with this view, but one cannot also ignore the atrocities committed in the name of democracy. To some extent, he is justified in writing that,

Nowadays “democracy” serves mainly as a sheepskin for leviathan, as a label to delude people into thinking that government’s ‘big teeth’ will never bite them [8].

People’s Participation

Theoretically, the essence of democracy consists in people’s participation in self-governance. That is why Abraham Lincoln’s most popular definition is universally accepted as ‘government of the people, by the people and for the people’. But this is all in theory only. It has only remained as delusory ideal. James Boward describes its functioning as largely an over glorified choice of caretakers and cage keepers [9].

Sometimes, democratic governments have behaved like 'lumbering giant bull-dozer'. 'We the People' has been a vacuous phrase, and in the name of supremacy of parliament this has been trampled. In actual practice, no government has truly been representative of people's will in toto. No form of democracy has been able to ensure all people's participation genuinely. In thought only in direct democracy, it is conceivable but in practice it has never been so. In modern times with large population, it is not feasible at all. What we have is not people's participation by themselves but through their representatives. But it is well known what sort of representatives they are, and how they manage to become representatives. For effecting representation generally adult franchise is used as a mechanism, but how it operates is also too well known. Boward [10] reports that Georgia legislature meets only forty days each year. Most representatives say that they have only weak familiarity with the policies they put into law. He cites observation of California State Senator H. L. Richardson who writes, '*Legislators consistently vote on legislation without understanding what is in it, especially when final vote is taken. Every legislature has his own system of judging how he will vote, but reading the bill usually is not part of the procedure*' [11]. Boward compares the functioning of representatives with 'two wolves and one lamb voting on what to eat for dinner' [12]. He quotes the opinion of John Cartwright who regards representation as 'poor consolatory word' [13]. The common opinion is that the pretensions of representative democracy are as hollow as that of bygone monarchs to 'serve the people'.

Rule of Majority

Democracy is considered as rule of majority, but how much is the percentage to form the majority is something to be pondered over. Less than half of the people are the voters, less than half of the voters show up for voting at the polls, less than half of the voters who show up understand the issues, and politicians themselves are often unaware of what lurks in the bills they vote for. It is difficult to ascertain majority and that apart majority is not always right. Not only there is 'illusion of majority rule', but measures are more often decided not according to the rules of justice or public well-being but by the superior force of interested and overbearing majority, silencing the minority even though it may be enlightened and right.

Rule of Law

Another feature of democracy is rule of law, but a distinction must be drawn between supremacy of 'an authority' and supremacy of a person or group of persons 'in authority', between 'law as sovereign' and 'law emanating from sovereign'. 'Rule of law' has been really a very attractive proposition, but it has proved to be utopian in democratic framework. Sometimes, freedom under law becomes freedom under leashes. The constitution can be said to be 'an authority', but it is quite often relegated to the background by the persons 'in authority' who become dictatorial. Imposition of 'emergency' in India by Mrs. Indira Gandhi can be cited as an example. Constitutions have been mutilated, suspended and overthrown, and laws have been misinterpreted mercilessly. It needs to be seriously thought over as to how to preserve and safeguard the supremacy of 'an authority' so that sanctity and functioning of constitution is not suspended or abrogated by powers that be who manage to be in authority.

Human Dignity

The hallmark of social progress and of civil society is respect for human dignity and human freedom within an ordered cosmos. This involves cultivation of values like liberty, equality, justice and fairness. It should be realized that each individual has immense potentialities and capabilities and should be given freedom and opportunities to manifest them. In different individuals, there are diverse capabilities and all are useful for social progress. Every human individual is a potential person and should be given scope to cultivate personhood. Personhood is an achievement concept. A person is one who is knowledgeable, ratiocinative, free and responsible being. He has to be an integrated, creative and freely acting social and moral being. He must know and realize the meaning of life, justify his/her existence and make it valuable and worthwhile for himself/herself and the society.

Fellowship

The criterion of social progress is realization of the spirit of fellowship, democratic mode of thinking and living and not just democratic form of state or political governance. Genuine democratic spirit prevails only when diversity is fully recognized and well accommodated in an overall unity. In the unity, differences are to be protected, preserved and enriched. They should receive natural and reasonable place and respect within the unity. Diversity is an outer expression of inner unity, like seed and tree. The unity in seed finds expression in various forms—the roots, trunk, branches, leaves, flowers and fruits and multiple seeds. All have different forms, colours and properties. Genuine democratic process should not be suppression of thoughts, feelings and aspirations of any section of people but their enfoldment and reinforcement. In other words, social progress has to be in the form of inclusive pluralism, having multiplicity well situated in unity like the organs surviving and thriving in an organism. In the ultimate analysis, there should be no difference between 'I' and the 'other'. On the front gate of Parliament House of the Republic of India in New Delhi, a verse from the traditional Indian culture is inscribed which states that the notions like 'This is mine or this is that of others' are nurtured only by persons of mean mentality and narrow mind. For broad-minded persons, entire universe is a family. The implication is that instead of viewing differences as 'I and the other' they should be viewed as 'I and ours'. The other is not to be regarded as an alien, an adversary, a competitor or a threat to one's existence but a partner, a companion, a fellow, an aid or help.

Democracy in Function

Democracy in all its present forms does not ensure any of the above-stated aspirations and requirements. In actual functioning, democracy in all its three wings of legislature, executive and judiciary is vitiated with multiple and incurable drawbacks, deficiencies and deformities. Though theoretically there is separation of powers among these three, often there are confrontations. Most deplorable has been the functioning of legislature, to which Gandhiji and Deendayalji have referred. To use Indian vocabulary, though Indian democracy is called *svarajya* (self-rule) it has never been *surajya* (good government). It is debatable whether democracy failed or people failed democracy. Even if it is granted that democracy in itself is good but we could not evolve suitable mechanism to practise it, and this also calls for rethinking about democracy. We have also to think going beyond democracy, if need be. Going beyond does not mean rejecting the basic spirit or merits of democracy. It only means rejecting all that is not good and beneficial, that which is detrimental to well-being and that which is harmful. It is only rejecting the darker side of it. At any cost, people's participation in self-rule, freedom of expression and rule of law are to be ensured. Important point is that we should at this juncture be willing to rethink the notion of political organization.

Jain Viewpoint

There can be several alternatives available. Modern Jain Acharyas propose that a good alternative can be sought and worked out from the age-old organic approach to understand the Reality and its manifestations in myriad social and political and other forms. The analogy of organism may be helpful in drawing out an outline of such an endeavour. It will be natural also as the order and harmonious functioning in an organism are built in it by nature itself. It has a sort of pre-established harmony, to use Leibnizian phrase. The whole organism, along with its multiple organs, functions smoothly in perfect coordination. It presents a model of peaceful coexistence, of harmonious functioning, of mutual care and share, and of multiplicity co-inhering in unity at both macro- and micro-levels. It is an apt and rich analogy that may profitably be harped upon.

In an organism, there is a built-in organization and no outside control and imposition, though there are external influences, some good and some bad. The good ones are to be assimilated, and bad ones are to be thwarted. There is no ruler-ruled relationship, no hierarchical order or authoritarianism in the functioning of organism. It is incorrect to understand that the cerebral system controls the nervous system unilaterally. There is supportive mutualism. Every organ in an organism functions in a natural way and contributes to the functioning of the total organism. The organism nourishes all its organs and is in turn nourished by each one of them. The functioning of organs and the organism is not rights-based. No one organ has any special privilege or position. The organs do not function in isolation or in collision. This is how the whole macrocosmic and microcosmic cosmos functions. In the cosmic process, everyone performs its assigned role dutifully and naturally.

This analogy has very interesting and promising implications for political thought. Some of the seminal ideas which can be attended in this regard are (a) corporate living with peace and harmony, (b) coexistence and cooperation, (c) collective functioning, (d) mutual caring and sharing, (e) self-regulation and self-control, (f) no demands for rights and privileges but only proper discharge of duties and obligations, etc. In organismic form of political organization, there is no governance but regulation. Everyone is equal, and everyone serves the other with mutual care and respect. Everyone acts in cooperation performing the role assigned in the social set-up. Though there will be no external authority, there will be a regulatory force and that will be a body of rules and regulations, checks and balances. There will be a set of rules and regulations 'in authority', but there will be no person or a group of persons as 'an authority' imposing their will from outside, a situation contrary to the present one. It will be rule of law and not of individuals. Equality, fraternity and intra- and intergenerational justice will be the guiding principles. This form of political organization can be termed as DHARMOCRACY or 'DARMATANTRA'. This was the ideal of ancient Indian polity where the king at the time of enthronement was required to take an oath that he would abide by dharma and serve as a servant of the people and not as a master. The concepts of 'rājā', 'nṛpa', etc., etymologically imply that even if it is rule by an individual he/she has to look after the happiness and well-being of the public who is under his/her protection and not to bother for self-interest. The goal of any human organization, political or otherwise, should be '*pālana*' which stands for maintenance, protection and promotion of the people. This is the rule of dharma. In this context, the analogy of pregnant woman is put forth who protects and nourishes the foetus in the embryo even at the cost of self-sacrifice. We find many statements in the Indian texts to this effect. Adherence to rules and regulations will be spontaneous and natural and not forced or imposed. Life has to be natural and spontaneous. It has to be in harmony with other existences. Coexistence, cooperation, reciprocity in help, mutual caring and sharing, etc., are hallmarks of a civil society. To talk of conflicts and clashes or to indulge in them is uncivilized, a decadence, a regression and a perversion. There has to be coexistence or confluence of cultures and civilizations. All regulations should be in the form of self-regulation. It means each one minding one's own business, each one taking responsibility for one's own actions, each one respecting the person of others and refraining from intruding into the lives of others. All this is possible through proper education of body, mind and will. This is what ethical teachings of seers and saints, particularly of the East, stand for. Thinkers like Mahatma Gandhi and others have argued for self-rule. In modern times, Dada Bhagwan, as he is lovingly and respectfully called, in his book 'Apta-vani' and Acharya Mahapragya, an eminent saint and scholar in his book 'Kaisi ho Ekkisavi Sadi? (What should be Twenty-first Century?)', have also argued for abolition of state control in favour of self-control and self-rule. They advocate cultivation of *dhārmika* individual, *dhārmika* society, *dhārmika* economy and *dhārmika* political order based on cooperation, non-violence, mutual trust and respect, mutual care and share, and universal responsibility. They appreciate the need for decentralization up to village level, not from top to bottom but from grassroot itself. If there can be self-regulation there will be no need of government, they maintain. To govern is to control, and to control is to coerce or to use force. It is said that if men were angels no government would be necessary. And why can we not make humans angels? Why can there be no moral and spiritual progress? Why should education not be human-making? Boward reports [14] that in the Montgomery County, Maryland, government sought to soften its image in 1985 by dropping the word 'government' from the County Seal, from government workers' business cards, and even from the slides of county government automobiles. County Executive Douglas Duncan justified the change by saying that the word 'government' was 'arrogant' and 'off-putting' and 'did not present the image of public service'. This was the situation in ancient India also, as has been reported in the booklet of Mahatma Gandhi 'Hind Swaraj' the report of Sir William Wedderburn Bart in the Appendix, and it may be reproduced here for our perusal. It runs like this,

> The Indian village has thus for centuries remained a bulwark against political disorder, and home of the simple domestic and social virtues. No wonder, therefore, that philosophers and historians have always dwelt lovingly on this ancient institution which is the natural social unit and the best type of rural life: self-contained, industrious, peace-loving, conservative in the best sense of the word.... I think you will agree with me that there is much that is both picturesque and attractive in this glimpse of social and domestic life in an Indian village. It is a harmless and happy form of human existence. Moreover, it is not without good practical outcome.

It is not that we have to imitate the past blindly, but it is good to be benefitted by revisiting the past. Of course, it is desirable that governance or political organization should be by the people but more basic is that it should be *for the people.* It must be kept in mind that any organization, political or any other, is for what and for whom. Peace within and peace outside should be the ultimate goal of all human endeavours. Peace and prosperity go together. Prosperity has to be a shareable good, and genuine prosperity is holistic and universal based on inter- and intragenerational justice. State and government are human institutions which can be made and unmade. They are for humans and humans are not for them. H. L. Mencken in 'Treatise on Right and Wrong' [15] writes,

'*The great failure of civilized man is his failure to fashion a competent and tolerable form of government*'. There has been a saying, 'That government is the best which governs the least'. If this is the case, then why crave for 'statism' and why not to seek alternative. There can be alternative in allowing people to lead their own lives, provided people are properly educated from very childhood in the ethics of self-regulation.

In fact, this organic model calls for a paradigm shift of values and structuring of a new set of suitable vocabulary. Some vocabulary like that of 'public servant' can be retained, if it helps. It further requires a suitable system of education, as the new value system is to be cultivated right from childhood. Education is the best and surest means available to humankind. How education can effectively mould the minds in right or wrong direction can be learnt from the experiments of dictatorial communist countries where minds of people are completely brain-washed. The way pet animals are trained and their mindset conditioned the same can be applicable to rational human beings who are more amenable to education and transformation. In the history, we have experimented with many forms of governance, even now we are experimenting with democracy and monarchy, and it is hoped that this model can also be given fair trial. But care is to be taken that the basic spirit and good features of democracy are not bartered. Only the deficiencies, drawbacks and pitfalls painfully experienced everywhere are rectified and removed. As the society progresses, human mind also develops the capacity of innovative thinking and therefore the question is, can we not think of a system better than democracy, a system in which all the merits of democracy are well preserved and demerits negated. Though we have come to stay with democracy as the so far available best form of political governance, this cannot be treated as the end of history. The rational and ingenious human mind should not entertain the idea of end of human reason or thinking capacity. It should be possible for the creative mind to grow, to move ahead and to evolve to think of a state higher and better than democracy, a state which encapsulates all the virtues of democracy and discards its vices and defects.

References

1. Hansard, November 11, 1947
2. Gandhi, Mahatma. (2001). *Hind Swaraj* (pp. 27–29). Ahamdabad: Navjivan Publishing House.
3. Ibid.
4. Ibid, pp. 29–30.
5. Ibid.
6. Upadhyay, D. D. (2018). *Integral humanism* (p. 4). Chitrakoot: Deen Dayal Research Institute.
7. James, Boward. (1999). *Freedom in chains* (p. 2). New York: St. Martin's Press.
8. Ibid, p. 3
9. Ibid, p. 4
10. Ibid, p. 112
11. Richardson, H. L. (1978). *What makes you think we read the bills?* (pp. 38–39). Ottawa: Carolina House.
12. James, Boward. (1999). *Freedom in chains* (p. 97). New York: St. Martin's Press.
13. Ibid, p. 100
14. Ibid, p. 26
15. Ibid, p. 213

Suggested Readings

1. Mahapragya, A. (1999). *Kaisi Ho Ekkisavi Sadi.* Ladnun: Jain Vishva Bharati.
2. Mahaprajna, A. (1994). *Democracy and social revolution through individual transformation.* Ladnun: Jain Vishva Bharati Institute.
3. Mahaprajna, A. (2002). *Ekkīsavi Śatābdi aur Jaina Dharma.* Ladnun: Jaina Vishva Bharati.
4. Mahaprajna, A. (2000). *Lokatantra: Nayā Vyakti, Nayā Samāja.* Ladnun: Jain Vishva Bharati.
5. Tulsi, A. (2013). *Religion, anuvrat and human wellness.* Delhi: Adarsha Sahitya Sangha.
6. James, B. (1999). *Freedom in chains.* New York: St. Martin's Press.
7. Bhagwan, D. (2015). *Aptavani.* Mumbai: Dada Bhagwan Foundation.
8. Faguet, E. (1912). *The cult of incompetence* (translated from the French by B. Barstow). New York: E. P. Dutton & Company.
9. Gandhi, M. K. (1928). *Young India.* New York: India Home Rule League of America.
10. Gandhi, M. (2001). *Hind Swaraj.* Ahamdabad: Navjivan Publishing House.
11. Pragya, S. K. (2014). *Acharya Tulsi kā Rāṣtra ko Avadāna.* Ladnun: Jain Vishva Bharati Institute.
12. Arora, R. K. (2008). *Ethics in governance.* Jaipur: Aalekh Publishers.
13. Upadhyay, D. D. (2018). *Integral humanism.* Chitrakoot: Deen Dayal Research Institute.

Chapter 12
Jain Theory of *Puruṣārtha*

Abstract It is said that human existence is the highest manifestation in the cosmic process. Yet human being is not perfect. He/she has immense potentiality to develop. The ratiocinative human being has the unique capacity and ability to undertake planned and purposive enterprises which are technically known as *puruṣārtha*. With this capability, human can overcome the adventitious imperfections and restore his/her pristine purity. This theory is related to the doctrine of *karma* which is central to Indian culture. It regulates human conduct as per the prescribed value schema. Its ultimate aim is spiritual perfection. It consists of gradual and graded realization of spiritual enhancement technically known as *guṇasthāna* which involves fourteen stages of development.

Keywords *Śramaṇa* · *Puruṣārtha* · *Mokṣa* · *Pañcasamavāya* · *Samvara* · *Nirjarā* · *Yoga-kṣema*

Introduction

Jainism as a part of *Śramaṇa* tradition puts forth *puruṣārtha* or self-help as a basic principle of authentic life, without looking for any help from supra-human agency. It is to be self-reliant (*svastha*, i.e. to be situated in one's own self, *svasmin tiṣṭhati*). It is to remain confined to *svabhāvaparyāya* or *svaparyāya* (to stick to one's own nature) and to be free from *vibhāvaparyāya* or *paraparyāya* (not to be perverted due to external influences) as far as possible. In the worldly life, it is very difficult to be so, but this is put forth as an ideal. The *jīva* (self) has to be unaffected by and unassociated with *ajīva*. This is the state of *mokṣa*. But we are worldly beings, and we have to be in association with and dependent upon other beings and material entities. So mutual affection and consequent affliction are unavoidable. All livings beings are mutually dependent. Likewise, the non-living entities also help us for our survival. So, we have a collective living (*samgha jīvana*). The cosmos is a vast and subtle networking of multiple and multifaceted but interrelated and interdependent existences are characterized by both permanence and change. The cosmic set-up is not mechanical or blind interplay of existences. It is teleological, purposive and goal-oriented. All happenings are causal happenings and not accidents or chance

S. R. Bhatt, *Jainism for a New World Order*,
https://doi.org/10.1007/978-981-33-4041-1_12

occurrences. But in the total set-up, human being has a unique and privileged position. He/she is endowed with the capacity to know the true nature of things, to act freely within some bonds and to be responsible for one's actions. He/she is partly free and partly determined but the determinations are also one's own making due to our *karmas*. Thus, Jainism takes into cognizance conducive or detrimental effects of the past actions and exhorts for management of actions and fruits of actions in terms of virtuous conduct and austere living.

Theory of *Pañcasamavāya*

In the causal happenings brought about by human agency, there are five causal factors the integrated conglomeration of which gives rise to an event. They are *bhāva* consisting of substance (*dravya*), place and circumstances (*kṣetra*) and time (*kāla*). They constitute material cause. The second is *puruṣārtha* (present human endeavour out of free will). The third is *daiva* or *niyati* or *prārabdha* (accumulated past *karmas* of the agent which have not so far fructified). The fourth is *kālalabdhi* (proper time conducive for production), and the fifth is *bhavitavyatā* (possibility of production of action) [1]. Among these five, *puruṣārtha* plays a dominant and significant role in so far as other factors are beyond human control but human conduct is solely dependent upon human free will, and it can be planned and managed. There is no incompatibility among these five factors, and that is why their integration is possible and it is known as *pañcasamavāya*. Samantabhadra in Āpta Mīmāmsā advocates their complementary character.

The theory of *puruṣārtha* offers a new rationality for a paradigm shift from exploitation to service, from hedonistic pleasure to spiritual enhancement. This is the *anaikāntika dṛṣṭi*. Another notable thing is that in this enterprise, there is scope for divine inspiration but there is no room for divine help. There is no God who is a saviour. The divine beings are there who can serve as catalysts or as ideals to emulate. Self-effort is the only means available to us for self-realization. The *daiva* is also our own making, and through virtuous conduct we can minimize or neutralize its effect. That is why practices of *samvara* and *nirjarā* are recommended. Thus, the Jain theory of *puruṣārtha* puts forth a pattern of planned, purposive and methodical endeavour for a rational, free and responsible human agent with proper management of modes of knowing and living and adequate regulation of will and effort. *Karma* or *puruṣārtha* determines the entire individual and social set-up of a person. Effects of *karmas* are different upon different individuals, and different *karmas* have different effects on the same individual in accordance with nature (*prakṛti*), duration (*sthiti*), intensity of fruition (*anubhāga*) and quantity (*pradeśa*).

In the worldly life, all existences are equally valuable and significant. This feeling leads to cultivation of *ahimsā* which is a foundation of collective and corporate peaceful living, a life of mutual caring and sharing, of interrelatedness and reciprocity. But this presupposes a well-regulated life with legitimate controls which should be self-generated. This partaking calls for corporate and cooperative efforts and just distribution and enjoyment of the fruits. So, the Jaina tradition shares the general Indian view of fourfold puruṣārtha, viz. *dharma*, *artha*, *kāma* and *mokṣa.*

In this world, every creature has to earn one's living. This is more meaningful for the rational, ratiocinative and responsible human being. He/she has to plan the performance purposefully. Then only it is authentic living. All social, economic and political organizations are established and aimed at this requirement. They serve human needs and requirements but are to be properly managed to serve the purposes for which they are established. But ultimately, all human endeavours and enterprises should be a means to and directed towards the realization of cosmic well-being which is the summum bonum of life. It a state of freedom in which infinitude of the self is restored. So, pursuit of *puruṣārtha* is needed here.

Theory of *Karma*

All individual selves in their pure form share the four infinite virtues. But in empirical state, they differ from one another. These distinctions are due to beginningless subtle material coverings known as *karma.* It has physical and psychical aspects known as *dravya karma* and *bhāva karma,* respectively. Though, of varied nature, *karma* has been broadly classified into eight types. They are as follows:

1. Knowledge-obscuring—(*jñānavaraṇīya*)
2. Intuition-obscuring—(*darśanavaraṇīya*)
3. Feeling-producing—(*vedaṇīya)*
4. Delusion-producing—(*mohaṇīya*)
5. Longivity-determining—(*āyu*)
6. Body-making—(*nāma*)
7. Status-determining—(*gotra*)
8. Obstruction-generating—(*ānataraya*)

The soul has to experience the fruits of good or bad karmas which it performs knowingly or unknowingly. There is no escape from them.

The summum bonum of life is realization of four infinites (*ananta catuṣṭayas*). This is known as *mokṣa* or *mukti.* The best and surest means of it is *yoga.* The technique of *yoga* symbolizes the core of Indian spiritual *sādhanā.*

Theory of *puruṣārthas* has been cardinal to Indian way of life. It has been formulated keeping in view the structure of the universe and the constitution of human person. Whatever be its formulation, it is commonly accepted in Vedic, Jain, Buddhist, Sikh and all other traditions. Along with a theory of *karma,* it is a salient and distinguishing feature of Indian culture.

Theory of *puruṣārthas* is based on two presuppositions. One is that the universe and the cosmic process are teleological, purposive and goal-oriented. There is a built-in telos in the cosmos. The other is that human being is the highest emergent so far in the cosmic process. It is finite but has the capacity to develop infinitely. There are immense potentialities inherent in human which can be manifested given suitable conditions. Human existence has meaning and significance but this can be realized only through right knowledge, proper planning and skilful endeavour. Theories of *karma* and *puruṣārthas* have been put forth only in this context.

Analysis of Concept of *Puruṣa* (Person)

Human being is the centre of all moral and legal reflections in so far as all moral and legal considerations are meaningful and applicable only in the context of human. The behaviour of inanimate objects or animals does not attract moral and legal evaluations. Even the behaviour of an insane or infant human is not an object of moral and legal pronouncements in the strict sense. This clearly implies that all moral and legal deliberations presuppose a particular view of human to whom alone moral and legal responsibility are attributable. There are certain properties possessed by human by virtue of which alone he/she becomes a proper and fit candidate for moral and legal evaluations. This is specifically the case in the moral context. *Puruṣa* means such a moral agent who is ratiocinative/discursive, who possesses freedom of will and who has a teleological or purposive outlook. In order to bring out full implications of this concept in a moral context, we may do well to dwell upon these properties of human, which are at once both constitutive and regulative. They constitute the nature of human but are not fully manifested in human. There has to be purposive, planned, methodical and regulated enterprise to realize those potentialities. The word '*puruṣa*' etymologically means one who strives for enhancement (*purati agre gacchati iti puruṣaḥ*). Hence, they are the ideals to be pursued and strived at by human.

The primary requirement of a moral agent is the capacity to discriminate between the good and the bad, the virtue and the vice (*viveka*), etc. No doubt ignorance of law cannot be an excuse, but the awareness of law and the prevalence of the conditions conducive to such awareness are a necessary precondition. A law cannot be adhered to unless and until one knows what it is, what is the means and what are the modalities to practise it. That is why moral and legal education should be an essential part of general education which should be imparted through both formal and informal modes of imparting education.

The second requirement of a moral agent is the possession of freewill. Every act is not a moral act. Acts like eating, sleeping, etc., do not come under the purview of moral evaluations as these do not involve a choice between good or bad, etc. Only such voluntary activities which are directed to bring about some desired fruits can be subjected to moral evaluations. In other words, the moral acts are the acts performed by such an agent to whom the responsibility of its performance can be attributed not only in terms of its formation but also in terms of owning up of the consequences. Thus, the theory of *karma* has both the attributive and the retributive aspects. This attribution of responsibility and the retribution of the consequences (*phala*) presuppose freedom of will in the agent and availability of alternatives in the given situation. *Karma* has distributive aspect as well since it is a collective enterprise for universal well-being, and *karmaphala* is necessarily to be distributed as just and fair play.

Human being is not only conscious but self-conscious as well. He/she has the painful realization that all is not well with the present existence. There is a constant feeling of imperfection and finitude. This is a hard fact of life which is undeniable. This is not a cause for pessimism but a call for enlightened activism. It stimulates and motivates a knowledgeable person to undertake planned and skilful performance.

In the performance of *puruṣārthas*, there are three steps of knowledge of the goal (*sādhya*), of the adequate and conducive means (*sādhana*) and of skilful employment of modalities (*itikartavyatā*). The basis of choice of goal is its appropriateness (*aucitya*). It is appropriate if it is conducive to individual and universal well-being (*artha* and not *anartha*), and it is realizable (not *asādhya*). The means has to be in accordance with the goal (*anukūla*). It should be available and accessible also (*upalabdha*). The modalities stand for proper knowledge and skilful employment of means (*upayakauśala*) to realize the goal. Since the modalities have to be composite, it is necessary to know the different steps and their priority and posteriority (*paurvāparya*) while undertaking the performance.

There is a quadruple principle underlying pursuit of *puruṣārthas*. It is *jñāna-icchā-kriyā-phala* (knowledge-will-effort-result). All these four are to be properly harnessed in their symbiotic interrelationship.

Puruṣārthas have to be collective and corporate enterprise. An isolated human individual never exits. He/she is a part and parcel of the total reality and has no existence or meaning apart from this totality. There is reciprocal dependence, supportive coexistence, judicious cooperation and mutual caring and sharing. Of course, it is the individual who is the agent but this agency is possible only in a collectivity, and therefore, the motives and intentions of every act should be the well-being of the collectivity. The Gītā ideal of '*loka samgraha*' is the guiding spirit of all theorizing about *puruṣārthas*.

As mentioned earlier, traditionally four *puruṣārthas* have been conceived and they are by and large accepted in all Indian traditions. But there is no fixity of number. What is important is that a human person should lead a planned life with proper knowledge and pursuit of proximate and ultimate goals of life. For this, there can be different patterns of theorizing but the fourfold traditional schema seems to be universally desirable.

In the fourfold schema, *dharma* is the foundation and guiding principle; *artha* and *kāma* are *preyas*, i.e. worldly goals for earthly well-being and *mokṣa* is *niḥśreyas*, i.e. beyond the two. *Dharma*, *artha* and *kāma* are to be pursued in the empirical life. *Mokṣa* is trans-worldly life in which all bonds of empirical existence are transcended. In Indian culture, we have *Dharmaśāstra*, *Arthaśāstra*, *Kāmaśāstra* and *Mokṣaśāstra* traditions each one having enormous expository literature. It is worthwhile to be acquainted with them, even though one may not wholly adhere to them.

This fourfold schema has been accepted in all Indian traditions. It provides meaning to human existence and offers guidelines to live a meaningful life. It contains symbiosis of empirical and trans-empirical both of which are essential aspects of human existence. It further caters to the material and spiritual dimensions of human life in their proper place and proportion. With suitable modifications, it can be universalized. The basic framework can be the same, and details can be worked out as per the requirements of time and place.

Suggested Readings

1. Amrtachandra, Puruṣārthasiddhyupāya, Srimadrajachandra Ashram, Agas
2. Mahendra, K., & Lal, Z. J. (1994). *Neuroscience and karma.* Ladnun: Jain Vishva Bharti Institute.
3. Samantabhadra, Āpta Mīmāmsā, Bharatiya Jnanapith, Delhi (2002)
4. Shah Nagin, J. (1998). *Jaina philosophy and religion.* Delhi: B. L. Institute of Indology.
5. Sogani, K. C. (1967). *Ethical doctrines of Jainism.* Sholapur: Lalchand Harichand Doshi.
6. Nathmal, T. (1951). *Studies in Jaina philosophy.* Jainashram-Varanasi: P.V. Research Institute.

Chapter 13
Jain View of Perfection

Abstract In the worldly existence, human life is imperfect and finite. It suffers from many limitations. But human being has the ability to be aware of imperfection and transcend imperfection. In him/her, there is innate inclination to do so. Human life is meaningful and aims at realizing the proximate and ultimate goals of life. This can be possible by planned and purposive effort at the individual and global levels. For this all cultures have to draw a value schema to be pursued. The value schema may differ from cultural to culture but fundamentally all should have basic commonality. All have to collaborate and cooperate in this enterprise.

Keywords Human life · Organicism · Spiritual globalization · Culture · Value schema

Introduction

Human life is a prized possession; the best outcome of cosmic process emerged so far. It has been a remarkable psychophysical fruition animated by spiritual principle. Self-consciousness and reflective awareness are its unique features. On the basis of his/her planned endeavour and successful behaviour, human being has been able to achieve wonderful feats. A mechanistic understanding of human ontology and human evolution cannot do justice to the spontaneity, creativity and goal-oriented human pursuits. The Reality is experienced to be through and through telos-embedded and human life being its part and parcel has to reflect this feature. Teleological approach alone can support a viewpoint that coordinates work and welfare, possession and enjoyment with a spirit of sacrifice, social progress and social justice, material well-being and spiritual enhancement. The cosmic process is an ongoing movement. It does not halt or wait. Nothing should be regarded as final, inevitable and conclusive at the present juncture. If it is turned and twisted in a wrong direction, it will keep on moving in that direction only. But if it is given a right turning and tuning, it can move in a desirable direction. It is for the free, rational and responsible human agent to choose the correct path and provide a right direction to the cosmic process. Here comes the role of knowledge, values and education under the guidance of spiritual reflections.

S. R. Bhatt, *Jainism for a New World Order*,
https://doi.org/10.1007/978-981-33-4041-1_13

Organismic Approach to Reality

Reality is symbiosis of unity and multiplicity. It is an organic unity, a multiplicity-in-unity, not unity brought about in or superimposed on multiplicity. Multiplicity is accommodated in an ordered way in unity and that is why it is cosmos and not chaos. It is universe and not multi-verse. It is universe in the sense that it houses many in one as parts of an organic whole. The Sanskrit words *jagat* (mutative world) and *viśva* (cosmos which pervades all) are suggestive of this fact. This is how the ontological issue of 'one' and 'many' is to be approached. Both one and many are inevitable facts of our experience. In a satisfactory position, both are to be recognized and accommodated in a holistic and integral system, in a synthesis, in which the two are not posed as opposites but as complimentary. The analogy of living organism, discussed earlier, is best suited to explain the nature of Reality. A living organism is neither an assemblage of scattered and unrelated multiple parts, nor is it a barren unity or an abstraction that is bereft of the multiplicity of its organs. It is a concrete unity that realizes itself in and through the multiplicity. Just as a part is not intelligible except through the whole of which it is a part and just as a whole is not conceivable without any reference to its constituent parts, so also the organs are not intelligible except as inhering in an organism, and the organism also is not conceivable without any reference to its organs. Thus, organicism regards one and many as members of an organic whole each having a being of its own but a being that implies a relation to the other. This is a holistic and integral approach based on the principles of interrelation and coordination, mutuality and cooperation, reciprocity and interdependence.

In no other system of thought, one can speak of such a world of mutual appreciation and organic interrelation and interdependence. In absolutism there is no manifoldness but solid singleness. In dualism, there is no mutuality but rigid bifurcation. In pluralism, there is no interrelatedness but monadic exclusiveness. So, these systems cannot entertain the idea of mutual give and take, mutual appreciation, mutual caring and sharing that is the core of organicism. The chief value of organicism is that it recognizes the inalienable individuality and the reality of manifoldness of finite spirits and matter and assigns them a proper place, function and value in the unifying framework of an all-embracing unity without in any way destroying its wholeness. The multiplicity is not annihilated but preserved and protected in the unity, derives its being, discharges its functions and realizes its value within the concrete unity. Both are necessary to each other and realize themselves in and through the other.

Like Reality, our experiences are also multifaceted and multi-layered. They have to be so in order to be genuine, veracious and comprehensive. The variety of experiences is in tune with multiplicity of Reality. Ordinarily, our experiences are sense generated. We possess cognitive senses that provide us variety of experiences, both internal and external. The functioning of cognitive senses is both amusing and bewildering and at times beyond the ken of human understanding. It also undergoes expansion and contraction with the increase or decrease of cognitive capacity. It can be thwarted by impeding forces and augmented and reinforced by supplementing agents. The ever-increasing scientific and technological inventions and advancements have devised many apparatuses that serve as aid to the enrichment of our experiences particularly of the objects that are remote, or subtle, or covered. There is constant and perhaps endless improvement in our cognizing capacity.

Further, there is something called supernormal cognition that opens up a new field of experience. It is a cognitive domain that is sometimes a suspect but its veracity cannot be out rightly rejected. Availability of such experiences to some gifted persons cannot be denied on the ground that they are not available to everyone or they are not available to ordinary senses.

The evolved human consciousness is bifaceted in so far as it is self-conscious as well as object conscious. We know, we know that we know and we also know that what we know is true and useful or not. On the basis of ratiocinative discrimination, we form judgements. We make a distinction between fact and value. These two are distinct but closely interrelated and interdependent. Fact is already in existence, and value is to be brought into existence through our efforts. Experience of facts enables us to postulate values and engages us in the pursuit of their realization. When a value is realized, it becomes fact. So, fact-value dichotomy is only apparent and for practical purposes only. Consciousness of values and their planned and systematic realization is another unique feature of human being.

Nature of the Universe

There is organic interdependence, cooperative partnership and supportive mutualism in community living in the universe. There is reciprocity between living beings and inanimate things. All living beings have to coexist in the universe but it has to be a regulated coexistence just like a nest (*niḍa*) of a bird, wherein the young ones coexist in a peaceful and regulated way. The bird–parents operate with the attitude of distributive justice and selfless sacrifice, and the young ones also coexist in mutual cooperation and cosharing. They do cry for food but do not quarrel with one another. The parents see to it that their needs are satisfied but they do not feed their greed. If little creatures can have such a harmonious living, why can we who claim to be rational not do so? So, the guiding principles of communitarian life are *sahavāsa*, *sahakāra* and *sahabhoga*. Entire cosmic existence is corporate coexistence, and therefore, human progress coincides with cosmic progress as well. There is inclusive pluralism with mutual cooperation and supportive partaking.

Nature of Human Existence

Human being like any other item of the cosmos is a divine spark. He/she is finite–infinite. He/she is potentially infinite. Basically, he/she is infinite conditioned as finite. Finitude is not his/her basic nature. He/she mistakes himself/herself to be finite. So, he/she has to restore his/her divinity and experience infinitude. His/her real self is pure consciousness and bliss which is named as perfection. This perfection is a matter of realization. But this realization will be only after attainment of ratiocinative knowledge of finitude. He/she has to know that he/she is not finite or imperfect and he/she has to transcend his/her finitude. To illustrate this point in the Jain tradition, a threefold state of human existence is described. It is given in the appendix at the end of this chapter.

In the worldly existence, human being is beset with ignorance and consequent bondage which is misery mongering. He/she hankers after worldly belongings which are evanescent and ephemeral. He/she has an inkling of perfection. He/she cherishes to be eternal and immortal but does not know what real immortality is. He/she mistakes mortal to be immortal and suffers when he/she realizes that which he/she took to be immortal has turned out to be mortal. Though the real self is perfection and infinitude, it suffers from cognitive, volitional and affective imperfections. In worldly existence, it is body–mind complex animated by the principle of spirit or soul. It is the spirit which is its real self. Body–mind complex is extraneous, adventitious and an imposition or covering. This makes it finite–infinite. This extraneous imposition has to be discarded. Then only real self can be experienced. But in order to experience the real self first, we have to know the empirical self which exists in this mutative world (*jagata*) having his or her own existential network (*samsāra*).

Holistic Understanding

We have the experience that apart from the physical, we possess vital, mental, intellectual and spiritual dimensions that are all equally important. They are all interrelated and mutually supportive. They are distinct but not separate and cannot be reduced to any one of them. They may have existential hierarchy from gross to subtle but they do not have value-based hierarchy as all are of equal value. Quality of life is to be attained in terms of catering to the legitimate needs of all these in a balanced and proportionate way. In fact, lopsided development of any one or a few of them is harmful to the total human person and is detrimental to perfection whatever be the degree of its realization. The physical, vital, mental and intellectual belong to the empirical world and can be approached with the help of sciences but the spiritual belongs to a different category. It is trans-empirical and beyond the ken of empirical sciences. There are therefore two realms of human existence, empirical (*vyavahāra*) and trans-empirical (*niścaya*), one constituting the base and the other the apex. Both are organically interrelated. Wise persons differentiate between the two but do not ignore one for the sake of the other. There can be priority and posterity or there can be simultaneity in their pursuits depending upon the situational requirements. But there is no chasm or gulf between the two. The spiritual is trans-empirical but it is not anti-empirical. Rather it is the fulfilment of the empirical. The empirical is a prerequisite and stepping stone for the trans-empirical. One cannot be realized without the other. There has to be a symbiosis of science pertaining to the empirical and spirituality pertaining to the trans-empirical, the former seasoning and tempering the latter and vice versa.

Human being is closely related to Nature, subhuman beings and other human beings. Human identity, therefore, is the totality and intricate unity of all these with subtle and fine internetting, interdependence and interaction of the three which constitute human personality. Added to this is the social dimension that is highly complex, complicated and subtle network of relations. Sociality is built in human nature and no human existence is possible and conceivable without society. Human beings themselves constitute society. Society provides the ground and sustenance for human existence and also the basic structure and materials for human evolution. So there is reciprocal interdependence. Human progress coincides with social progress. But there is no dichotomy or chasm between individual existence and social environment. All social organizations are means for collective progress. If a particular form of social organization is not fully conducive to this goal, there should be innovative changes and transformation.

Progress as Evolution (:) Banking on Tradition and Rooted in Culture

Change is the law of reality, but it has to be a change for the better, for more perfect, for greater well-being. All change is not necessarily healthy and good. In order to be beneficial, it has to be in the form of evolution rather than revolution. It must be based on the solid foundations of the past, its experiences, concerns and commitments. But this process of bringing forward from the past requires a judicious discrimination as to what should be accepted and what should be rejected.

This brings us to the consideration of tradition. Tradition makes a person and society and, contrary wise, a person and society make a tradition. So, there is mutuality between the two. Similarly, change and modernity do not mean breaking away from the past experiences. What is needed is a correct understanding of the nature and role of tradition. In Jain, philosophical thought emphasis is laid on utilization of past experiences as also experiences of others. Tradition is an embodiment of values and norms handed down from the past. It is never a threat to individual and social freedom unless it is dead, dated and outlived. It contributes to the discovery of meaning of life. Cultural life consists in pursuit and realization of values that enhance quality of life of human being and his/her society. Therefore, culture has to enrich, enlarge and encourage fullness of life, delight of mind and plenitude of peace. There can be no genuine progress without cultural backing and cultural regeneration preceding and consolidating it.

Human being possesses the capacity of innovative creativity. Culture is shaped and reshaped by creative human consciousness. In creative consciousness, past experiences are relived and renewed. It is also previewing the future. Re-enacting the past, enlivening the present and visualizing the future are tasks of a dynamic culture. Here past, present and future coalesce into one. The present envelops the past and contains the seeds of the future. In this respect, the present occupies a pivotal place, as it is a symbiosis of the actual and the potential. A living culture renders past contemporaneous and makes the contemporary as foundation of the future.

Goal of Human Life and the Cosmic Process

The pursuits of excellence, striving for betterment and attainment of quality of life have been perennial human concerns and aspirations. All human endeavours in diverse fields of culture and civilization have been directed towards realization of this goal. Freedom from imperfection and consequent suffering have been the chief motivating factors for all cognitive enterprises and technological advancements. Though every human being cherishes and strives for these and posits them as goal of life, their realization requires planned corporate efforts. It cannot be a single individual enterprise. A single individual may work out a plan but its execution has to be collective. Moreover, this goal implies attainment of excellences and best possible quality of life not only of the individual but also of the entire cosmos since the two are interrelated and interdependent and constitute an organic whole and therefore also it calls for collective efforts. This apart, one cannot attempt to realize a good quality of life keeping in view an isolated individual, society, nation or region. It has to be a global vision and a universal realization without any prejudice to any one section of the universe. Everyone has to participate and partake in the fruits of this venture that is a collective enterprise. Everyone should be able to contribute by manifestation of one's capabilities through a dynamic discovery of one's potentials being assisted in this process by the society and natural surroundings. So when we plan for social progress, our outlook should be global though our performance has to be at the local level. Genuine social progress consists in the realization of universal well-being, in a sense of care and concern for all, a feeling of oneness with all, an attitude of sharing and cooperating.

Need of Global Human Endeavour

The notions of 'perfection', 'peace', 'harmony', 'goodness' and 'quality of life' have been projected and nourished in different cultural traditions of the world so that all that is true, good and beautiful, which is worth reckoning and emulating, may be brought together and synthesized for pursuit of individual happiness, social progress, world peace and cosmic well-being. These are the ideals cherished by the humankind at all times all over the world but they have always been elusive from effective realization. In the context of present-day quest for globalization and universal harmony in the strife-ridden and divided world, such a renewed attempt may help in generating conducive climate and congenial mindset through proper and adequate education and other media of mass communication. Thought motivates action, and good thoughts will certainly ensue in good deeds. It is pragmatic to live by ideals even though they may not be easily or fully realizable. They are not to be in the form of utopia but attainable through human endeavour. Ideals need to be projected and pursued. There have been seers, sages, saints and knowledgeable persons in every known historical age and in every region, who have on the basis of their subliminal intuitions given us noble ideas and ideals for universal welfare. It is prudent to go by their precepts and practices that have eternal relevance and utility.

Quality of Life and Spiritual Globalization (Vasudhaiva Kuṭumbakam)

Quality of life in its perfect and highest form is the summum bonum of human existence, and globalization is its corollary since its realization requires propagation, profession and practice of global ethics. The principle of 'universalizability of ethical norms' and adherence to them without exception stem from this very consideration. But globalization is not to be understood in materialistic terms only in the sense of liberalization of trade and commerce. Basically, it is a spiritual ideal. It is inculcation of the attitude of seeing self-sameness everywhere leading to global unity. It is realization of fundamental unity of the entire cosmos, not just of human beings or living beings. It is a mode of cosmic coexistence with a spirit of mutual support, mutual sacrifice, mutual caring and sharing. It is an enlightened conduct and contented life like that of a bodhisattva or jīvan mukta who is constantly engaged in universal well-being, who is happy in the happiness of others and feels miserable in the miseries of others, who always thinks of good of others and acts for their welfare. The seers and sages, spiritual and religious leaders, all over the world have enjoined this mode of living. The moral codes prescribed in all the cultural and religious traditions in all ages and places aim at cultivation of this mindset of universal affinity and self-sameness. We possess vast literature in this regard but human nature is such that it has to be constantly reminded about this and persuasively goaded to practise this. This accounts for the need and relevance of the present endeavour.

Spiritual globalization is not monopolistic patenting or bulldozing of multiplicity in overt or covert form but accommodating and harmonizing it within the organic unity of the entire cosmos. It stands for coordination rather than uniformity of thought and action. It envisages no antagonism or incompatibility between one part and the other, like one organ and the others in an organism, since all are perceived and conceived as interconnected, interrelated and interdependent elements of one and the same whole constituting a single field or continuum or unity. That is why analogy of a living organism is put forth where there is 'multiplicity-in-unity' (not 'unity-in-multiplicity), many situated in one, not as separated, segregated and scattered elements, but in mutual openness and reciprocity supplementing and complementing one another. Here conflicts and disorders may not be unnatural but their resolutions and harmony may also not be unrealizable.

Mode of Achieving the Goal

Such a globalization is a viewpoint and a course of action, a policy instrument and a worldwide movement for a new world order based on enlightened principles of conduct aiming at enhancement of 'quality of life' not just of human beings but of the entire cosmos. This calls for newer formulations of global ethical norms that may regulate the entire gamut of human conduct in relation to one human being and another and also between human beings and the rest of the cosmos of multiple animate beings and inanimate things. This is the precursor of the emergence of a global society in which the entire world can be experienced as one single family. This is possible through the realization of self-sameness and cultivation of the spirit of sacrifice. But this necessitates a trans-valuation of values, a paradigm shift in values, a changed mindset, an enlarged vision of cosmo-centricity, an enlightened view and way of life by a proper training of body and mind by illuminating knowledge and liberating wisdom. It calls for a total transformation of matter and mind and realization of spiritual oneness. It is widening of the self as totality, from 'I' to 'We', from one self to total self, from individual to cosmic. Here there should be no deprivation and exploitation, no sorrows and sufferings that are unmitigated, no injustice and discrimination unabated. This is realization of heaven on earth, to use figurative language. The cosmos is full of splendours and can provide sustenance to all its inhabitants but we have to ensure that this is done in a just, fair and equitable manner. But this is possible only through the postulation of a new value schema other than the one we are presently pursuing. It is the restoration and reformulation of the classical value schema that we have forgotten. It is practice of new ethics that tends all and cares for all. This has been the cherished desire of the enlightened mind. It is not a utopian dream but an ideal realizable in actual practice through proper and adequate education.

Value Schema for Individual and Social Progress

Quest for perfection and realization of values of life that reflect meaning and purpose of our existence has been perennial human concerns. Any consideration of such value schema should be based on concrete social and historical realities and past experiences of the concerned individual and society. Values are not just to be known and posited, and they are to be realized as well and lived in action. This calls for a symbiosis of knowing, doing and being.

There can be no realization without skilful means. This implies cataloguing of resources, preserving and enhancing the existing ones and generating new ones without depleting the existing ones. Skilful employment of means also implies judicious use of the resources without depriving others of the present generation and the future generations. It further implies proper management of action and the fruits of action with equitable and just distribution.

Holistic and Integral Approach to Progress

A meaningful planning for progress has to be all-round, graded and gradual realization with balance and proportion. Economic progress is basic to human progress but economic aspect is only one of the multiple aspects and cannot claim exclusive attention. Human development is not to be confined to economic development, and mere economic development cannot be equated with human development. Further, in order to ensure just and equitable partaking in the fruits of economic progress, it should be dharmic in nature regulated by 'business ethics'. No doubt pragmatism and utilitarianism are the guiding principles of economics, but they should be seasoned and tempered by welfarism. Unbridled economic growth gives rise to moral crises, and many problems crop up which may seriously imperil society and its health. It may appear to be a growth but it may not be conducive to well-being. There has to be value orientation of economy in tune with human well-being and cosmic welfare. Economy has an instrumental worth, and it should not be taken as an end in itself. It is also to be remembered that not only economic development is to be guided by morality; it should also help in enhancing moral capacity. Morality should not remain confined to precepts but should get translated into practice.

Science, Technology and Social Progress

Like economy, science and technology are important components of human culture. Science directs technological innovations, and technology accelerates progress of science. Both are thus interdependent. Both are needed and are essential to human existence and social progress. But they are not value neutral. They should serve the ultimate human good that is also the cosmic good. They are means and therefore of instrumental character. They should be humane and humanizing and should be harnessed for social progress and cosmic well-being. They should not be allowed to technocalize human being; rather they should be humanized. In this respect, a clear distinction should be drawn between humanism and humanitarianism. Humanism is anthropocentric and is vitiated by human fallenness, whereas humanitarianism is cosmo-centric. Only by spiritual orientation of science and technology, they can be made humanitarian. Such an orientation can come from traditional culture. At present, there is a see-saw between traditional culture and science and technology instead of a thaw. There is a need for 'great harmony'.

Whatever is stated here in a general way holds good in the context of Jainism when reinterpreted in modern setting. It is hoped that the ideas propounded here may find favour with modern mind. These are the implications of Jain scriptures.

Appendix

According to Jainism, the souls are of three types on the basis of the states of their existence, (i) conditioned and embodied (*bahirātmā*), (ii) awakened and indwelling (*antarātmā*) and (iii) pure and supreme (*paramātmā*). The embodied soul is that which is identified with the body and the senses and the outer objects. The awakened is the indwelling soul which is self-aware. The supreme soul is the one who is free from all *karmic* taints. He/she is divine. The embodied soul has perverted vision and is devoid of real knowledge. The awakened has right vision and right knowledge. The supreme soul is devoid of all attachments, is omniscient and pure. Brahmadevasuri, in his commentary on Bṛhaddravyasamgraha-14 states that '*Atra bahirātmā heyaḥ, upādeyabhūtasya anantasukhasādhakatvāt antarātmā, paramātmā punaḥsākṣādupādeya ityabhiprāyaḥ.*', i.e. 'The *bahirātmā* is appalling and to be discarded. The *antarātmā* is to be resorted as it gives infinite bliss. *Paramātmā* is to be ultimately realized'.

The summum bonum of human life is attainment of the state of *paramātmā* after passing through the state of *antarātmā* and renouncing the state of *bahirātmā.* These are the three stages of spiritual evolution. Human being looks outward before he looks inward, and he looks inward before he looks upward. The *bahirātmā* sees outward, the *antarātmā* first turns inward and then moves upward which is the consummation of spiritual journey. Every individual self is potentially divine, and manifestation of divinity is *paramātmapada.* This is the terminus of spiritual development which consists in renouncing the external self and realizing the transcendental self by means of the internal self. This is known as *Śuddhopayoga.* According to Kundakunda, it consists in relinquishing the *bahirātmā* and by turning to the *antarātmā*, and reaching to the *paramātmā* through the medium of *dhyāna.* ('Mokṣa Pāhuḍa' 4.7.) These three states of self are to indicate the need to discriminate the 'self' and 'not self'' and to chalk out the path to spiritual perfection.

The tripartite classification of human beings goes back to Kundakundācārya (see selections from his Atthapāhuḍa in the Samanasuttam, Gāthā, 178&9) who writes,

Jīva havanti tivihā bahirppā taha ya antarappā ya.

Paramappā vi ya duvihā arahantā taha ya siddhā ya

Akkhaṇi bahirappā antarappā hu appasaṅkappō

Kammakalaṅka vimukkō paramātmā bhaṇyate dēvaḥ

Muniraja Yoindu (Yogindu) in Paramātmaprakāśa (2–5, 90–6) elaborates this threefold distinction. In Yogasāra (6–11), also he discusses this point.

On the basis of classical Jain literature, Prof. K. C. Sogani in his book 'Ethical doctrines of Jainism' (pp. 168–70) discusses the characteristics of these three states as follows:

> The characteristics of the bahirātmā may, in the first place, be accounted for by affirming that he identifies himself with the physical body, the wife and children, silver and gold etc. with the logical consequence that he is constantly obsessed with the fear of self-annihilation on the annihilation of body and the like. Secondly, he remains engaged in the transient pleasures of the senses, feels elated in getting the coveted things of the unsubstantial world, and becomes dejected when they depart. Thirdly, he is desirous of getting beautiful body and physical enjoyment in the life hereafter as a result of penances, and is tormented even by the thought of death.
>
> Antarātmā stands for the spiritually converted self who has relinquished eight kinds of pride and considers his own self as the legitimate and genuine abode, esteeming the outward physical dwelling places as unnatural and artificial. Secondly, he renounces all identification with the animate objects like wife, children etc. and with the inanimate objects like wealth, property etc., and properly weighs them in the balance of his discriminative knowledge. Thirdly, by virtue of sprouting of profound wisdom in him, he develops a unique attitude towards himself and the world around him. His is the only self that has acquired the right of mokṣa and consequently he adopts such attitude as is necessary to safeguard his spiritual status, and the interest he gets endowed with such type of insight as will enable him to make spiritual invasion resolutely and then sound the bugle of triumph after defeating the treacherous foe of attachment and aversion assaulting him in his bahirātmā state.
>
> Paramātmā is the Supreme self, the consummation of aspirant's life and the terminus of his spiritual endeavours. He is free from impurities and defects. He possesses infinite knowledge, bliss and potency. It is realization of Self's svarūpa sattā. Ācāraṇga says that Supreme Self is ātmasamāhita (self-contained) but all pervasive. Yogindu (Paramātmaprakāśa, I.41) proclaims that the universe resides in the Paramātmā and the Paramātmā resides in the universe but He is not the universe.
>
> Paramātmā is pure self, antarātmā is converted self and bahirātmā is perverted self. Bahirātmā is enveloped in mithyātva which is corruptive of knowledge. Antarātmā is awakening of consciousness of the transcendental Self. Paramātmā is pure self. Bahirātmā is in spiritual slumber, antarātmā is awakened self and paramātmā is the enlightened self. The spiritual potentiality of antarātmā gets actualized in paramātmā. Bahirātmā accepts worldly objects as his own, antarātmā negates them and Paramātmā transcends them.

This spiritual journey consists of fourteen stages known as guṇasthānas in which there is spiritual conversion or transformation at every stage.

In Prof. Sogani's book referred to above we, find a very illuminating comparison between the Jain and Vedāntic conceptions of *paramātmā,* pointing out their similarities and differences (pp. 207–16). He also dwells in a comparative account of Jain and Vedāntic conceptions of *bahirātmā* and *antarātmā* (pp. 218–20).

Prof. Nathamala Tatia in his book 'Studies in Jain Philosophy' (pp. 281–2) explains that this tripartite distinction is done in the Jain tradition in the context of *dhyāna* as a means to spiritual development leading to self-realization. He writes, *'The Jains, like others in the field, put stress on self-realization. The materialist view of the self as identical with the body is the first thing that one is to get rid of in order to tread the path of spiritual realization. For this purpose one is required to turn inward and concentrate upon the self as distinct and separate from the body. When one is fully convinced of the distinction between self and not-self, one is required to rise still higher and concentrate upon and realize the transcendental self which is free from all the limitations of the empirical self. Acharya Kundakunda and, following him, Pujyapāda and Yogindudeva have very thoroughly discussed this method of self-realization in their respective works* viz. *Mokṣaprābṛta, Samādhitantra and Paramātmaprakaśa. They distinguish three states of the self* viz. *the exterior self (bahirātmā), the interior self (antarātmā), and the transcendental self (paramātmā). The self with the deluded belief that it is none other than the body is the exterior self. The self that clearly discriminates itself from the body and the sense organs is the interior self. The pure and perfect self free from all limitations is the transcendental self. The exterior self becomes the transcendental self by means of the interior self. Or, in other words, the transcendental self is the self-realization of the exterior self through the intermediary stage of the interior self. The self or the soul is intrinsically pure and perfect. Its limitations are due to its association with karmic matter. Considered from the point of view of gunasthana, the soul before it cuts the knot (granthi) and experiences the first dawn of the spiritual vision is the exterior self, and the soul after the vision and before the attainment of omniscience is the interior self. On the attainment of omniscience the self becomes the transcendental self. One is to eradicate the interior as much as the exterior in order to realize the transcendental self. This process of eradication is yoga*'.

The conclusion is that *bahiratma* is the defiled, sullied, bound and impure self. But it has the potentiality of becoming pure and infinite and can enjoy its unalloyed status of bliss. So the self has to elevate itself and realize *Paramātmapada* via *antarātmā*.

Further Readings

1. Bhatt, S. R. (2018). *Concept of Parmātmā, Antarātmā and Bahirātmā—A comparative analysis*. Surat, Gujrat: Vitrag Vignan Charitable Research Foundation.
2. Mahendra, K., & Lal, Z. J. (2015). *Samayasāra*. Ladnun: Jain Vishva Bharati Institute.
3. Sogan. K. C. (1967). *Ethical doctrines of Jainism*. Sholapur: Lalchand Harichand Doshi.
4. Nathmal, Tatia. (1951). *Studies in Jaina philosophy*. Varanasi: P.V. Research Institute.

Glossary

Āhāra nourishment
Ahimsā non-violence
Ananta dharma infinite properties/qualities
Anekāntavāda doctrine of non-absolutism
Anekānta dṛṣṭi perspectival multiple view
Anukampā compassion
Anumāna inference
Anuprekṣā self-contemplation
Anuṣṭhāna spiritual activity
Aṇuvrata moderate vows/an ethical movement
Apāya passions
Apramattasaṃyata complete self-restraint
Apratyākhyānakriyā harbouring passions and possessiveness
Aprigraha non-possessiveness
Ārjava straightforwardness
Ārambhakriya acts damaging the environment,
Asaṃkyeya countless, innumerable
Āsrava karmic inflow
Asat unreal
Ajīva non-sentient entity
Ajñāna/Avidya ignorance/delusion
Bahuparigraha extreme possessiveness
Bandha bondage
Bhāva himsā mental violence
Bhaya fear
Bodhi enlightenment
Buddha the enlightened one
Cāritra conduct
Caritrācāra ethical code
Caturdaśaguṇasthāna fourteen stages of spiritual development

S. R. Bhatt, *Jainism for a New World Order*,
https://doi.org/10.1007/978-981-33-4041-1

Dāna beneficence, charity
Dayā compassion
Dharmavidhi spiritual mode of living
Dhārana retention
Dhyāna concentration/meditation
Dravya substance
Dravya himsā physical violence
Dukkha/Duḥkha suffering
Dveṣa hatred
Ekānta-mithyā-darśana absolutist deluded view
Guṇa quality
Guṇavrata subsidiary vows
Guṇasthāna state of spiritual development
Guru preceptor
Hetu cause
Heya worthy of abandonment
Himsā violence
Himsāvirati abstinence from violence
Icchāparimāṇa limitation of wants
Icchājayi victor on wants
Ihā speculation
Indriya senses
Indriyapratyakṣa sensory perception
Jina victor over passions
Jijñāsā inquisitiveness
Jīva conscious being
Jñāna wisdom
Kāla time
Kleśavimokṣa freedom from passion
Karuṇā compassion
Kaṣāya passions
Karma karmic material particles
Kevalajñāna omniscient knowledge
Krodha anger
Kuśala virtuous or wholesome
Manas mind
Mithyādarśana deluded world view
Mokṣa/Mukti liberation
Naya partial standpoint
Nirodha cessation
Nisarga-kriyā approving of an evil act
Nitya eternal
Pāpa harmful karma/sin
Pāramārthika transcendental
Paramāṇu atoms

Parokṣajñāna mediate knowledge
Parārtha for others
Pratikramaṇa to retreat
Prāṇa bioenergy dependent upon biopotentials
Parigraha possessiveness
Parigraha parimāṇa limitation of possessiveness
Parigrahasamjñā instinct of possessiveness
Parigrahakriyā possessive clinging
Parigrahavirati abstinence from possession
Paripūrṇa perfect
Pariṇāma transformation
Paryāya mode
Paryāpti biopotential
Prabhā lustre
Prajñā wisdom
Pramāda dereliction/carelessness
Pramāṇa right mode of knowing/holistic perspective
Pramātā knower
Prameya object of knowledge
Pramiti authentic knowledge
Pratyakṣa immediate knowledge/perception
Pratyaya causal condition
Praśama calmness
Pramāṇa approved means of knowledge/holistic knowledge
Pudgala matter
Puruṣārtha planned and purposive human effort
Puṇya beneficial/merit
Rāga attachment
Rasa taste
Śabda sound
Sahabhoga mutual care and share
Sahakāra/Sahayoga cooperation
Sahavāsa/Saha-astitva coexistence
Sakala whole
Sambhava probability
Sama tranquillity
Samatva vision of equality
Samādhi meditation
Samaṣṭi group
Samudaya causal origination
Sāmānya universal
Sāmayika abstinence from all sinful acts
Saṃkalpa intentions/determination
Saṃvara stoppage of influx of karma
Saṃskāra memory traces

Smṛti memory
Saṃsāra cycle of birth and death
Saṃvyāvhārika empirical
Saṃyama self-restraint
Saṃyoga conjunction
Samyakcāritra enlightened conduct
Samyakjñāna enlightened knowledge
Samyakdarśana enlightened view/right faith
Śānta tranquil/peaceful
Sat existence
Satya truth
Sīla virtuous conduct
Siddha pure soul
Śoka sorrow
Saptabhangi sevenfold predication
Smṛti recollection
Śruta spiritual knowledge/verbal testimony
Steya stealing
Śubha auspicious
Śuddha pure
Sūkṣma subtle
Sukha happiness
Svabhāva intrinsic nature
Svārtha for one's own sake
Tamaḥ darkness
Tapas austerity
Taijas luminous
Tarka reasoning
Tattva real entity
Tīrthaṃkara founder of religious doctrines/adorable Jain seers
Tyāga renunciation
Upkāra beneficence
Utpāda origination
Vācya expressible
Vaivāvṛtya selfless service
Vedanā pain/distress
Vicikitsā doubt regarding action
Vikala part
Viparyaya opposite/deluded knowledge
Vīrya energy
Vītarāga one who is free from passions
Viśeṣa particular, specific
Vivakṣā intention for speaking
Vyaṣṭi individual
Vikalādeśa partial/limited view

Vyaya cessation
Vyutsarga abandoning
Yathārthajñāna true knowledge

Bibliography

A

Acharya, M. (2006). *Samāja Vyavasthā ke Sūtra*. Ladnun: Jaina Vishva Bharti.
Acharya, M., & Kalam, A. (2008). *The family and the nation*. Delhi: Harper Collins Publisher.
Acharya, M. (Ed.). (1994). *Ācāro Bhāṣyam*. Ladnun: Jain Vishva Bharati Institute.
Acharya, M. (2001). *Anekānta: Reflections and clarification*. Ladnun: Jain Vishva Bharati Institute.
Acharya, M. (2005). *Anekānta, Ahimsā aur Śānti*. Delhi: Adarsha Sahitya Sangha.
Acharya, M. (2001). *Anekānta: View and issues*. Ladnun: Jain Vishva Bharati Institute.
Acharya, M. (2002). *Anekānta: The third eye*. Ladnun: Jain Vishva Bharati Institute.
Acharya, M. (1999). *Bheda Mein Chipā Abheda*. Ladnun: Jain Vishva Bharati Institute.
Acharya, M. (1994). *Democracy and social revolution through individual transformation*. Ladnun: Jain Vishva Bharati Institute.
Acharya, M. (2006). *Ekānta mei Anekānta*. Ladnun: Jain Vishva Bharati Institute.
Acharya, M. (2002). *Ekkīsavī Śatābdi aur Jaina Dharma*. Ladnun: Jaina Vishva Bharati.
Acharya, M. (2008). *Happy and harmonious family*. Ladnun: Jain Vishva Bharati.
Acharya, M. (2000). *Jain Darśana aur Anekānta*. Churu: Adarsha Sahitya Sangha.
Acharya, M. (2008). *Jain Darśana: Manana aur Mīmāmsā*. Churu: Adarsha Sahitya Sangha.
Acharya, M. (2000). *Lokatantra: 'Nayā Vyakti, Nayā Samāja*. Ladnun: Jain Vishva Bharati.
Acharya, M. (1994). *Astitva aur Ahimsā*. Ladnun: Jain Vishva Bharati.
Acharya, M. (1984). *New dimensions in Jaina logic*. Ladnun: Jain Vishva Bharati.
Acharya, M. (2004). *Philosophical foundation of Jainism*. Delhi: Adarsh Sahitya Sangha.
Acharya, M. (2003). *Samasyā ko Dekhanā Sīkhe*. Delhi: Adarsha Sahitya Sangha.
Acharya, M. (2003). *The quest for truth*. Ladnun: Jain Vishva Bharati Institute.
Acharya, M. (2008). *Vigyāna Adhyātma ki Aur*. Ladnun: Jain Vishva Bharati Institute.
Acharya, M. (2009). *Training in non-violence*. Jaipur: Gulab Kaushalya Charitable Trust.
Acharya, M. (2010). *Anekanta: Philosophy of Co-existance*. Ladnun: Jain Vishva Bharati Institute.
Acharya, M. (2003). *I and Mine*. Ladnun: Jain Vishva Bharati Institute.
Acharya, M. (Ed.). (2006). *'Ātmā kā Darśana*. Ladnun: Jain VishvaBharati Institute.
Acharya, M. (Ed.). (2002). *Suyagado*. Ladnun: Jain Vishva Bharati.
Acharya, M. (2005). *Economics of Mahavira*. Delhi: Adarsha Sahitya Sangha.
Acharya, M. (2008). *Yugin Samasyā aur Ahimsā*. Delhi: Adarsha Sahitya Sangha.
Acharya, T., & Nathmal, Muni. (1974). *Aṅga Suttāni*. Ladnun: Jain Vishva Bharati.
Acharya, T. (2013). *Religion, anuvrat and human wellness*. Delhi: Adarsha Sahitya Sangha.
Acharya, T. (1996). *The vision of a new society*. Churu: Adarsha Sahitya Sangha.

S. R. Bhatt, *Jainism for a New World Order*,
https://doi.org/10.1007/978-981-33-4041-1

Acharya, T. (1950). *Jaina Siddhānta Dīpikā*. Sardarsahar: Adarsh Sahitya Sangha.
Acharya, T. (2001). *Bhagwana Mahavira: Life and philosophy*. Ladnun: Jain Vishva Bharati Institute.
Acharya, T. (Ed.). (2007). *Bhikṣu Nyāya Karṇikā (Bṛhadvṛtti)*. Ladnun: Jain Vishva Bharati.
Acharya, K. (1994). *Samayasāra*. Ajmer: Digambar Jain Samiti.
Acharya, K. (1984). *Pravacanasāra*. Agas: Rajachandra Jain Shastramala.
Akalankadeva, N. M. K. (Ed.). (1999). *Tattvārtharājavārtika*. Delhi: Bharatiya Jnanapith.
Amritachandra. (2019). *Puruṣārthasiddhyupāya*. Portland, USA: Generic Publishers.

C

Chaitanya, P., & Samanta, S. K. (2015). *Jainism in modern perspective*. Ladnun: Jain Vishva Bharati Institute.
Chaitanya, P., Narendra, B., & Kachhara, N. L. (2017). *Scientific perspectives of Jainism*. Ladnun: Jain Vishva Bharati Institute.
Chaitanya, P. (1992). *Scientific vision lord Mahavira*. Ladnun: Jaina Vishva Bharti Institute.
Chapple, C. (2006). *Jainism and ecology*. Delhi: Motilal Banarsidass.
Chapple, C. (2002). Jainism & ecology—Non-violence in this web of life. Harvard: Harvard University Press.
Chapple, C. (2001). The living cosmos of Jainism: A traditional science grounded in environmental ethics. California: Loyola Marymount University.

D

Dinesh, M. (Ed.). (2005). *Ātmā kā Darśana*. Ladnun: Jain Vishva Bharati.
Dixit, K. K. (1978). *Early Jainism*. Ahemedabad: L.D. Institute of Indology.

G

Galera, M. (2002). *Science in Jainism*. Ladnun: Jain Vishva Bharati Institute.
Galera, M. (2009). *Jain studies and science*. Ladnun: Jain Vishva Bharati Institute.
Glasenapp, H. V. (1942). *Doctrine of Karman in Jain philosophy*. Varanasi: P.V. Research Institute.

H

Hemachandra, S. S. (Ed.). (1989). *Pramāṇa Mīmāmsā*. Ahmedabad: Saraswati Pustak Bhandar.
Haribhadra, S. (2002). *Śāstravārtā Samuccaya*. Ahmedabad: L.D. Institute of Indology.
Haribhadra, S. (1942). *Anekānta Vijaya Patākā*. Baroda: Oriental Institute.
Haribhadrasuri, J. M. K. (Ed.). (1981). *Ṣaddarśana Samuccaya*. Delhi: Bharatiya Jnanapith.

J

Jinendra, V., & Sagarmal, J. (Eds.). (1999). *Samana Suttam*. Delhi: Bhagwana Mahavira Memorial Samiti.
Jinabhadra, D. M., & Bechardasji. (Eds.). (1968). *Viśeṣāvaśyaka Bhāṣya*. Ahmedabad: L.D. Institute.
Jain, C. R. (1999). *Jainism and world problems*. Bijnor: Jaina Publishing House.
Jain, D. (1997). *Pearls of Jaina wisdom*. Varanasi: Parshvanath Vidhyapeeth.
Jain, H. (2004). *Contributions of Jaina religion to Indian culture*. Ahmedabad: Sharadaben Chimanbhai Educational Research Centre.
Jain, J. P. (1944). *Religion and culture of the Jains*. Delhi: Bharatiya Jnanpitha Publication.
Jain, S. (1999). *Multi-dimensional application of Anekāntavāda*. Varanasi: Parsvanath Vidhyapitha.
Jian, S. (1988). *Jainism in global perspective*. Varanasi: Parsvanath Shodhpitha.
Jain, S., & Pandey, P. (2002). *Ahimsā ki Prāsangikatā*. Varanasi: Parsvanatha Vidyapitha.
Jain, K. (1983). *The concept of Pañcaśīla in Indian thought*. Varanasi: P.V. Research Institute.
Jain, K. (2018). *The applied philosophy of Jainism*. Shajapur: Prachya Vidyapeeth.
Jaini, P. (1979). *The Jaina path of purification*. Delhi: Motilal Banarsidass.
Zaveri, J. S., & Muni, M. (1994). *Neuroscience and karma*. Ladnun: Jaina Vishva Bharati Institute.
John, K. (1990). *Roots of conflicts, conflicts resolution through non-violence*. Delhi: Concept Publishing Company.

K

Kalghatgi, T. G. (1983). *A source book of Jaina philosophy*, translation of Devendra Shastri's, Jaina Darśana kā Svarūpa. Udaipur: Sri Tarak Guru Jain Granthalaya.
Kumar, A. (2005). *Jain Darśana Mein Anekāntavāda: Eka Pariśīlana*. Jaipur: Shri Digambara Jain Atisaya Ksetra Mandir.
Kothari, D. S. (1977). *Some thoughts on science and religion*. Delhi: Shri Raj Krishen Jaina Charitable Trust.

L

Lane, D. A. (2016). Ahimsā: A brief guide to Jainism. California: Mount San Antonio College.

M

Matilal, B. K. (1981). *The central philosophy of Jainism*. Ahemedabad: L.D. Institute of Indology.
Mehta, T. U. (1993). *Path of arhat : A religious democracy*. Varanasi: Naya Sansar Press.
Mehta, G., & Shah, K. (2012). *Various facets of Samana Suttam*. Mumbai: Somaiya Publications.
Mookerjee, S. (1978). *The Jaina philosophy of non-absolutism*. Delhi: Motilal Banarasidass.
Muni, N. (Ed.). (1971). *Āyāro*. Ladnun: Jain Vishva Bharati Institute.
Muni, N. (Ed.). (1976). *Thānam*. Ladnun: Jain Vishva Bharati Institute.
Muni, M. M. (Ed.). (1991a). *Uttarādhyayana Sūtra*. Beawar: Agam Prakashan Samiti.
Muni, M. M. (Ed.). (1991b). *Sūtrakṛtāṇga*. Beawar: Agam Prakashan Samiti.

Muni, M. M. (Ed.). (1995). *Prajñapana Sūtra*. Beawar: Agam Prakashan Samiti.
Munishri, N. (1998). Jaina Daśana. In N. J. Shah (Tr.), *Jaina philosophy and religion*. Delhi: Motilal Banarasidass Publisher Pvt. Ltd.

N

Nagin, J. S. *Jaina theory of multiple facets of reality and truth*. Delhi: Motilal Banarasidass Publisher Pvt. Ltd.
Nathmal, M. (1967). *Uttarādhyayana: Ek Samīkṣātmak Adhyayana*. Calcutta: Jain Svetambar Terapanthi Mahasabha.
Narayana, R. (2003). *Ecology and religion: Ecological concepts in Hinduism, Buddhism, Jainism, Islam, Christianity and Sikhism*. Delhi: Deep & Deep Publications.
Kachhara, N. L. (2018). *Living systems in Jainism: A scientific study*. Indore: Kundakunda Jnanapitha.
Kachhara, N. L. (2014). *Scientific explorations of Jain doctrines*. Delhi: Motilal Banarasidass.

P

Pujyapada. (2005). *Sarvārthasiddhi*. Delhi: Bharatiya Jnanpith.
Padmarajiah, Y. J. (1963). *Jaina theories of reality and knowledge*. Bombay: Jain Sahitya Vikas Mandal.

R

Rankin, A., & Shah, A. K. (2008). *Social cohesion: A Jain perspective*. London: Diverse Ethics Ltd.
Ramjee, S. (1992). *Jain perspective in philosophy and religion*. Varanasi: Parshvanath Shodhpitha.
Rampuria, S. C., & Rai, A. K. (Eds.). (1996). *Facets of Jain philosophy, religion and culture: Anekāntavāda and Syādvāda*. Ladnun: Jain Vishva Bharati Institute.
Rankin, A. (2018). *Jainism and environmental philosophy: Karma and the web of life*. London: Routledge.
Rankin, A., & Shah, A. (2018). *Jainism and ethical finance: A timeless business model*. London: Routledge.
Rankin, A. (2019). Jainism and environmental politics. London: Routledge.
Reading, M. (2019). *The anuvrat movement: a case study of Jain-inspired ethical and eco-conscious living*. Switzerland: MDPI Journal.

S

Siddhasena. (2000). *Sanmatitarka*. Ahmedabad: L.D. Institute of Indology.
Suri, V. (1967). *Pramāṇanayatattvālokālamkāra*. Bombay: Jain Sahitya Vikas Mandir.

Suri, M. (1970). *Syādvād Mañjari*. Agas: Paramasruta Prabhavaka Mandal.
Samantabhadra. (2002). *Āpta Mīmāmsā*. Delhi: Bharatiya Jnanpith.
Shastri, I. C. (1990). *Jaina Epistemology*. Varanasi: P.V. Research Institute.
Sikdar, J. C. (1991). *Jain theory of reality*. Varanasi: P.V. Research Institute.
Singhvi, P. (1999). *Anekāntavāda as the basis of equanimity, tranquility and synthesis of opposite view points*. Ahmedabad: Ārsva International Educational and Research Foundation.
Samani, M. P. (2005). *Jain Āgama mein Darśana*. Ladnun: Jain Vishva Bharati.
Sangave, V. (1999). *Aspects of Jaina Religion*. Delhi: Bharatiya Jnanapith.
Sadhvi, S. (1999). *Jñāna Mīmāmsā, Nandīsutra ke Sandarbha me*. Ladnun: Jain Vishva Bharati.
Schubring, W. (1962). *Doctrines of the Jainas*. Delhi: Motilal Banarsidass.
Sethia, T. (2004). *Ahimsā, Anekānta and Jainism*. Delhi: Motilal Banarasidass.
Sogani, K. C. (2001). *Ethical doctrines in Jainism*. Solapur: Jain Sanskriti Samrakshak Sangh.
Stevenson, S. (1970). *The heart of Jainism*. Delhi: Munshiram Manoharlal.
Sukhalalji, P. (1988). *Essence of Jainism*. Ahmedabad: L.D. Institute of Indology.
Shah, P. (2009). *Jainism: Religion of compassion and ecology*. California: Jain Education Committee.
Sims, L. E. (2016). *Jainism and nonviolence: From Mahavira to modern times*. Ohio: Cleveland State University.
Samani, K. P. (2014). *Acharya Tulsi kā Rāṣtra ko Avadāna*. Ladnun: Jain Vishva Bharati Institute.

T

Tatia, N. (1971). *Jainology and Ahimsā*. Vaishali: Vaishali Institute Research.
Tatia, N. (1951). *Studies in Jaina philosophy*. Varanasi: P.V. Research Institute.
Tatia, N. (Tr.). (2007). *Tattvārthasūtra: That which is*. Delhi: Motilal Banarsidass.
Trelinski, B. (2010). *Deep ecology and Jainism: Critical assessment of theory and practice*. Canada: Queen's University.
Tucker, M. E. (2018). *Routledge handbook of religion and ecology*. London: Routledge.

Lightning Source UK Ltd.
Milton Keynes UK
UKHW020652100122
396903UK00005B/300

9 789813 340435